Reading Your Writing

What Handwriting Reveals About You,
Your Relationships,
and Famous People Throughout History

Reading Your Writing

What Handwriting Reveals About You,
Your Relationships,
and Famous People Throughout History

GLORIA HARGREAVES

Quality Paperback Book Club
New York

Reading Your Writing

The Lover's Handbook

Handwriting and Personal Relationships

To Phillip and Danielle

CONTENTS

INTRODUCTION

One in three marriages in this country now ends in divorce and one in four adults lives alone, frequently not from choice. Why is it that our relationships so often turn out to be unsuccessful? Are our expectations too high? Do we give too little and ask too much? Are we unable to recognize and work through problem areas? Or have we chosen the wrong partner in the first place?

People can modify their behaviour and attitude, but fundamental character change is much more difficult. So it is unlikely that someone who is not compatible with you in the beginning will become so later. But relationships that worked well once can work well again, given under-standing and some effort on both sides. In a good relationship we allow our partner to grow, develop and mature; in a bad one both partners are likely to feel trapped and stifled. While there is no such thing as a *perfect* relationship, most of us can make the one we have as good as possible if there is a mutual wish to do so. To achieve this it helps greatly to have some insight into our own character and needs as well as those of our partner.

Handwriting analysis can here be of enormous assistance. It can show us ourselves as we really are and pinpoint problem areas in our relationship that may have become even more tangled through repeated arguments. For example, you may be accusing your partner of being intolerant, selfish or over-sensitive without realizing that you have your fair share of the same traits. At the same time you may be missing many positive qualities in your partner or yourself that you have not been aware of, let alone valued.

This handbook shows you how to spot positive as well as negative traits in your own and your partner's handwriting and provides you with the information you need to work out detailed character portraits of you both. Nothing could be simpler than reading, and noting, the interpretations that apply to your individual scripts and checking them against the many original handwriting samples illustrating the movements that are characteristic of different traits. While this will almost certainly result in some unexpected discoveries, it should lead you to a greater understanding of each other and offer you a better basis on which to build a future.

AIDS is with us now and is likely to be around for a long time. Trying to find happiness with your existing partner makes sense. Also, children suffer greatly when a relationship breaks up, so it is well worth exploring every avenue before taking the drastic measures entailed by separation or divorce. And it is a fact that most of us carry our existing problems into the next relationship or, alternatively, find a whole new set awaiting us. So pick up a pen and paper – and if possible get your partner to do the same – to see how you can help yourselves now. *Handwriting does not lie.*

1

How Reliable Are You?

Reliability and emotional stability are indicated by the *baseline* – the invisible line at the base of the middle-zone letters. A straight, even line demands control and will-power and is a good indicator of emotional adjustment.

baseline

STRAIGHT

I am . twenty eight of age and have been up for the same company

Your mind controls your emotions. You are a reliable partner. A good trait.

WAVERING

To live in the woods, to roam the hills and valleys, to soar over the foam

Your morals are a bit flexible. You should not let others influence you so much.

VERY ERRATIC

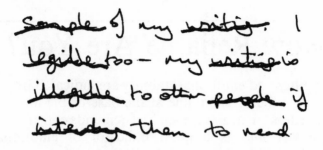

You are lacking in backbone and moral strength and are likely to be indecisive, unreliable and confused. You'll love them and leave them.

EXCESSIVELY RIGID

The time was near & she kn
hard bed of the Abbey guestha
stranger had stood in shadow.

You are over-controlled and frightened of letting others penetrate your thoughts. You can be explosive if control is lost.

WORDS RISING

difficult to write 'normally' w
are that someone will be

You are excitable, optimistic and easily aroused.

WORDS FALLING

is there any any
? Such, nowhere known some
li or braid or brace
re catch or key to keep...

If done occasionally, indicates tiredness. If done repeatedly, a sign of depression.

2

Are You an Extrovert or an Introvert?

The *size* of your writing shows how much value you place on yourself and how much you wish to impress others. The larger the writing, the more extroverted the personality. The very small writer will be more introverted and modest. Size should be measured from the top of the upper-case letter to the bottom of the lower-case letter.

writing 3mm / 3mm } 9mm / 3mm

The examples below show the three dominant sizes:

large size
9½ mm upwards

medium size 9 mm

small size 8½ mm or less

' very diplomatic and
ed Smaller type face
ne portrayed thereabouts-
Sizeable different and
I can really go to
es, which flows with

One thing is certain, life is never boring with these writers. Their greatest aim is to impress all around them. They seek recognition, and if you are not prepared to acknowledge in public how wonderful they are, you might as well give up now. They have great imagination and many leadership qualities. They enjoy working on large-scale projects, so don't ask them to replace the missing tile in the bathroom – they are much more likely to decide to redesign the whole of the ground floor. Minor details bore them, so it will help if you enjoy finishing off what they start! Their range of interests and activities is very wide – anything from amateur dramatics to golf – and you may have to resign yourself to playing second fiddle. Their optimism and enthusiasm never waver. They get enormous pleasure from buying extravagant gifts when the mood takes them. They are mainly cheerful partners. Sexually they have bags of imagination and generally the energy to convert it into practice. On the negative side, they can easily get bored and need a stimulating partner.

MEDIUM

I've always wanted to be come a vet. I was just wandering what qualifications you needed.

Thanks

These writers are basically realistic and down-to-earth, and neither over- nor underestimate their own worth. They show a high degree of adaptability and, on the whole, make good partners who can adapt well to either the large or the small writer. They tend to buy totally appropriate gifts and enjoy a reasonable amount of entertaining. Their range of interests tends to harmonize with the amount of free time available. Sexually they are pretty undemanding but, with encouragement, very open to suggestion!

SMALL

Apologies for not writing sooner. After reading Sze's letter, dreams of going over to London were dashed. My disappointment was compounded? by the numerous unsuccessful interviews. Now, I'm very upset because my parent and relatives are against me working as a front office cashier. And because of this, I couldn't concentrate fully during work, hence now, I owe the hotel around $400 due to an oversight/carelessness on my part, letting the guest checked out without paying for the room charges and forgetting to imprint (blank) the VISA card account number on the charge form. The hotel has already written to the

These are the more introspective types who hate the limelight. Frequently shy, modest and retiring, they relate best to people they know well, so don't fill the house with strangers and expect a jolly time. Invite a few close friends and they will be at their happiest. Any jobs around the house that require close attention to detail will be welcomed. They don't part with their money lightly (unless it's for a special offer that promises them a saving). You are likely to receive occasional small, well-chosen gifts, but don't expect anything too extravagant. Many small writers have considerable executive ability but they are the thinkers, not the doers. Sex will not be madly exciting – more ritualistic, considered and caring.

3

How Emotional Are You?

Loops are known as the avenue of the emotions and they tell us a great deal about our responses.

Do you understand your partner's emotional needs? There can't be anything more crushing than to say, 'I love you' and be met by a deathly silence. Perhaps your partner would like to respond warmly but experiences great difficulty in doing so. Yet repressing our emotional needs can make us feel angry and frustrated, so it's important for both parties to understand what those needs are.

VERY WIDE

Great emotional need is shown here. Although a lot of problems can arise if both partners have excessive needs, it is essential to allow these needs to be expressed. This can be tiresome as, once encouraged, you could be opening the floodgates. But it is vital for emotionally needy people to have a listening ear, otherwise they might seek an alternative outlet!

AVERAGE

Evidence of emotional well-being. These writers get enough feedback in their relationship and feel happy and contented within it.

RETRACED OR NARROW

l k b

A lot of inhibition is shown here, indicating great difficulty in freely expressing feelings, even when encouraged. These are the types who will say, 'Didn't I tell you last year that I love you? Why do you want to hear it again?'

STRAIGHT STROKES

Loved

When the loop has been eliminated completely, we find sound judgement and a tendency for the head to rule the heart. These people do not have a great need to seek emotional support. They make very loyal partners and are often amazed when *their* partners complain that they are not receiving the emotional support *they* need.

MIXTURE OF STRAIGHT STROKES AND LOOPS

lovely

This is normally a good combination. Although these writers may have different reactions to the same situation on different occasions, they seem to have the understanding and intelligence to appreciate the other person's point of view. The mixture is often found in the handwriting of partners who have a satisfactory relationship.

In conclusion, when partners have very different loop formations, it is important to recognize these differences in order to understand the other person. Often this is half the battle towards accepting them.

4

How Much Energy Do You Have?

The degree of *pressure* you place on your pen shows how much energy you have available for your goals, pursuits and sex life. How do you rate?

Heavy

Medium

Light

Pasty

Feel the back of the paper with your thumb and index finger to test for pressure: strong indentation equals heavy pressure; slight indentation equals medium; no indentation equals light; pasty, which looks heavy, has no indentation. It is frequently produced by a felt tip or broad nib.

HEAVY

These are demanding types, both emotionally and physically. We always know when they are around. They are forceful and need to make an impression, easily excited and quick to respond. They can also be very stubborn and, on occasion, morose. If you want a fun time and a very active sex life, this is the partner for you – that is, if you have a high energy level yourself!

MEDIUM

The majority of us fall into this category, with sufficient energy to get by on a day-to-day basis. These writers show a healthy degree of vitality and will-power. Sexually they are neither over-ardent nor passive. On the whole, they make nice, considerate partners.

LIGHT

A lot of sensitivity is shown here, as well as some delicacy of feeling. These are very idealistic types who often feel disappointed with their fellow men. They are impressionable and can easily be dominated by a heavy-pressure writer. Their will-power is a little weak, energy levels are low, and there may be a tendency to think of sex as unclean. They are however quite good at role-playing, so dressing up has a certain appeal!

PASTY

These are very sensual types, warm natured and good humoured. They have a deep appreciation of new ideas and situations, see the whole world as colourful and are frequently artistic. They welcome tactile stimulation and are sexually very experimental. On the negative side, they do like change and variety. If your partner is one of these types, hang on to him or her! Playing helpless is a good idea here – they love the underdog.

5

How Decisive Are You?

The way you form your letters – from angular to rounded – reveals a lot about how decisions are taken in your relationship. There are five different *letter formations*.

ANGULAR

12 May 1986

s dismissed by the British
sterday as being in the
in some cases
lusions of its report
rents ranging from
h flower remedies were
and negative by

You are highly intelligent, determined and mentally aggressive. You are also very good at sorting out major problems in your personal life, but run a mile when faced with minor difficulties or irritations. Human emotions tend to baffle you. You make a sexy, demanding, energetic partner.

GARLAND

"special" pen, and [a]
great pleasure from the
choices one has in
- making.

You are passive, non-competitive and delightful, but you have difficulty in asserting yourself. Always willing to lend a helping hand, you could easily allow yourself to be treated like a doormat by a dominating personality. Home, family and friends mean a lot to you and you are very hospitable. As you have a strong need for security, you are responsive to a considerate partner but completely crushed by an aggressive one, as you hate conflict. You would experience great difficulty in sharing your life with an angular writer.

ARCADE

[dre]ssing is not the right career
[on]e. I leave my present
[positio]n Hairdressing at the end of
[the mo]nth. I am now looking for
[a new] career and wondered what
[you co]uld tell me through my
[w]riting and my career decision

You express emotion in a very controlled way, do not welcome too much change and need the support of a reliable, caring partner. Socially you are a traditionalist but inwardly there lurks a bit of a rebel. You can be somewhat secretive, hiding a lot of your true feelings and thoughts. You take time to reach decisions but, once made, you stand by them firmly. Very loyal in relationships, you make a good, honest partner who gets along with most personalities.

THREAD-LIKE

after waiting
to think of
what one is going
to say. But when

You are somewhat unpredictable and can be difficult to pin down when decisions have to be made. You are very intuitive and love the arts. You are kind to your fellow men and look for appreciation rather than material gain, but you often feel unsure of yourself. High intelligence is shown, but you do not always know how to communicate it. As a partner you can be difficult, but you are always interesting. If the threading appears only at the end of a word, you are a born diplomat and negotiator.

ROUNDED

Basically, I am forever changing my career plans. One day, I am adamant that teaching is the career for me, and the other,

Hard work does not appeal to you much. You find it difficult to get down to a job and have some lazy days. Decisions are put off until the last possible moment and you would much rather let others make them for you. Nevertheless, you have a lot of charm, you are kind to others and always willing to offer a helping hand – provided this does not call for too much energy!

6

Do You Have a Jealous Nature?

Jealousy is a most destructive trait. It can cause untold damage even in an otherwise good relationship. Here are some of the main indications:

Jealousy

'a' AND 'o' LARGER THAN OTHER LOWER-CASE LETTERS
A sure sign of someone who feels insecure with his or her partner and demands their full attention – otherwise outbursts might occur.

H M n m

SMALL STARTING CIRCLE AT BEGINNING OF CAPITAL OR LOWER-CASE LETTER
Shows jealousy directed towards one particular individual.

H M m n

LARGE STARTING CIRCLE AT BEGINNING OF CAPITAL OR LOWER-CASE LETTER
Shows jealousy towards a number of different people. Writers who produce this movement will complain about the amount of time given to their partner's employer, hobbies, etc.

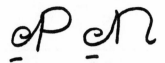

LARGE STARTING CIRCLE ON BASE OF CAPITAL LETTER

Used by people who will put obstacles in your way to prevent you from giving time to anything other than their needs.

7

Are You Clear-Thinking or Confused?

Spacing between lines is a measure of mental clarity and orderliness.

ONE LINE TANGLING WITH THE NEXT

People who write like this are often lively and forceful but they have difficulty in ordering their thoughts. Their concentration is bad and they don't find it easy to plan or organize anything. Confusion reigns. If you are organized yourself, these types could drive you insane. They are often stingy.

GOOD, CLEAR SPACING

ld I go back to my original
/ should I make a complete
a fresh caieei? My name is
twenty two years of age.

These are orderly thinkers who have the ability to explain things to others. Their writing shows good powers of concentration, flexibility and personal harmony. They make good committee members. They also enjoy organizing the family.

VERY WIDE SPACING

Today in the nicost weekend
that I've experienced in
many a day.

Although clear-thinking, these people are not able to communicate their ideas. They are usually distrustful of other people's motives and find it difficult to relate socially. They can be extravagant on their own behalf and occasionally generous to others. Basically withdrawn and quite isolated, they often feel different from the rest of the world and construct grandiose ideas for themselves.

8

How Truthful Are You?

Do you always tell the truth, find it easy to tell a 'white lie', or readily resort to lying? *Ovals* like 'a' and 'o' tell us a lot about how truthful we are in general and how much of ourselves we reveal in our personal relationships.

CLOSED

You think before you speak, and you tell the truth. You are basically quite reserved in your speech.

OPEN TO RIGHT

You are quite talkative and speak the truth directly to the person concerned. You despise liars.

OPEN TO LEFT

You have a strong tendency to talk behind others' backs and have been known to embroider the truth.

OPEN WITH KNOTS

You utter the first words that come into your mind and they are often far from the truth.

LOOPED AND KNOTTED

Even when it would be easy for you to tell the truth, you tend to tell white lies.

KNOTTED ON LEFT

You take pleasure in lying and enjoy deceiving others.

KNOTTED ON RIGHT

Lying has become such a habit for you that you can't even remember what the truth really is.

NARROW AND KNOTTED

You are selective in what you tell your partner and often lie by omission.

FINAL STROKE TO LEFT

A very self-protective sign. It indicates that you always have a quick answer to hand and are able to 'bend' the truth.

OPEN AT TOP

You are talkative but honest and sincere.

BROAD AND CLOSED

You are broad-minded. You let others have their say and also make a good listener.

NARROW AND CLOSED

You are frightened to speak the truth and frequently remain silent.

9

How Well Do You Communicate Your Feelings?

Slant – the angle of writing in relation to the baseline – is an indication of the way we relate to the world and reveals a great deal about our ability to communicate thoughts, feelings and needs to others. Slant can be divided into the following categories:

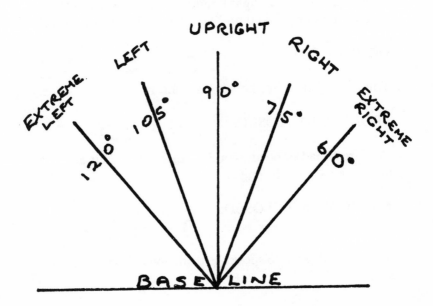

fully recovered show
of Trainee Chef, o
change and start
Denise and I'm
Please can

These are the most reliable of all types, with a head-ruling-the-heart emotional attitude. They can be difficult to catch but, being extremely loyal, rarely let you down once they are committed. They do not welcome great public displays of affection but a courtesy peck is quite acceptable. They enjoy sex with the one they love and suffer great pangs of guilt if they stray.

RIGHT

I am not for a moment
teaches or nurses for
Would do me same

These are emotionally healthy individuals with a fair degree of sensitivity, in the main sympathetic and compassionate. They can be reasonably demonstrative but won't encourage great outward displays of affection. Right slanters need a permanent partner as they have a lot of affection to give and like to plan for the future. They make good marriage partners. When it comes to lovemaking, they do like to take the initiative!

EXTREME RIGHT

is known and chosen to feel that my outlook or large and would like to be noticed.

These are types who cry and laugh very easily. They love a weepy film and are suckers for hard-luck stories. They are quick to react – with either elation or dejection. Being in love is a constant trait of their personality, from the age of nine to well into the nineties. On the negative side, they cannot always decide where their true affection lies: it could be with you or with your best friend! They find it difficult to keep their hands off the opposite sex.

LEFT

So far we are enjoying our trip to Norway, meeting people ... as Gloria and looking forward to your letter on ...

Caution is the name of the game here. On the surface these people are extremely charming, but they find it very difficult to commit themselves emotionally to anyone on a long-term basis. Once committed, though, they are yours for life. They tend to have rather unforgiving natures, so don't let them down! They also dislike last-minute changes of plan. Their mothers can be very important to them, so you could well find yourself part of a threesome. They also enjoy visiting museums, art galleries and old buildings, and talk a lot about the past. They can make very good lovers but may need some encouragement along the way.

EXTREME LEFT

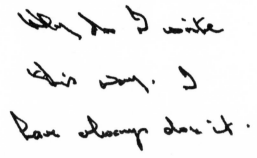

This is fairly uncommon, but if you do meet one of these writers you will notice at once how evasive he or she can be. People in this category have extreme difficulty in expressing their emotional needs or in understanding yours. They tend to marry late in life and never really form a close relationship. Being excessively sensitive, they are quick to take offence. Life is never easy with an extreme-left slanter. In bed, the partner will need to take most of the initiative.

ERRATIC

If you want to make yourself unhappy, marry one of these! They will love you today and leave you tomorrow. Often they make interesting and amusing companions, but not on a long-term basis. Communicative one day and silent the next, you never know where you are with them. They have been known to leave you at the altar! Sexually they are frustrating types, rearing to go one minute and claiming exhaustion the next.

10

Are You Logical or Intuitive?

Do you connect every letter, find it difficult to connect any letters, or come somewhere between the two? The way we make *letter connections*, or fail to do so, is related to how logical or intuitive we are. If one partner relies mostly on logic and the other largely on intuition, this can create misunderstandings and problems. How do you rate in this area?

totally connected

totally disconnected

some disconnections

TOTALLY CONNECTED

not that I'm not confident but I know that if I don't have to do any work then I don't! I have the basic ability but have always hoped (and teachers have said) that there

These are logical, systematic thinkers who are stimulated by a mental challenge. They strongly dislike being interrupted in any task they have undertaken and will always wait until they have reached an appropriate stopping point.

Socially they can be inconsiderate and tactless. They enjoy solving other people's problems, especially when they have not been invited to do so. On the other hand, they are not too good at solving their own, because the closer they are to something the greater their difficulty in seeing it clearly.

They are not particularly sympathetic people – unless you are suffering from an ailment they too have suffered from. Then they are likely to go on about it at great length.

Sexually they tend to think of what has happened in the past or what might happen in the future, so they completely miss what is going on now. Any appeal made to this kind of person must be based on logic. So keep your emotions under control!

TOTALLY DISCONNECTED

I am a 17 year old student wi

I am stuck between to ambitior

the opposite I would like to be

I was reading this article ar

Could tell me what type of co

These are the intuitive types whose opinions spring from feeling rather than reasoning. Occasionally they come up with brilliant ideas, but they often need help putting them into practice. Their minds could be described as being of the grasshopper variety!

They have strong likes and dislikes, so not everybody you introduce them to will be warmly received. They can be moody and restless, and may appear vague.

On the positive side, they are very sympathetic and often play 'Agony Aunt' to others while retaining a strong sense of their own individuality. Sexually they are inclined to call the tune but, when in the mood, they are interesting and imaginative lovers.

SOME DISCONNECTIONS

Down in a deep dark ditch sat

old cow munching a beanstalk.

Here we have the best of both worlds – a combination of
logic and intuition. These people keep on a fairly even keel:
they are not as compulsive as the totally connected writer,
nor as restless and moody as the totally disconnected one.
They handle their problems well and are sensitive to the
needs and wishes of others. This makes them very good
friends and lovers, with a healthy appreciation of their own
and their partner's sexual needs.

11

How Do You Act in Social Situations?

Broadness or narrowness in your letter formation is an indication of how you behave in a social situation. Are you socially outgoing or shy and self-conscious?

BROADNESS

[handwriting sample]

Broad writers are expansive in social situations. They love mixed company and are quite happy to allow their partners to circulate freely and talk to whomever they please, never feeling neglected if they are not included. They have a great sense of adventure and enjoy travel, feeling excited from the moment they start packing. They love open spaces, new places, walking, rambling and other outdoor pursuits. They also like large rooms in which they can spread themselves. They talk easily and enjoy change and variety in their friends and colleagues. All this makes them good hosts who love spending money on clothes, food and wine – sometimes to the point of extravagance.

With no inhibitions in their personal relationships, these types are easy to be with. Their sense of adventure and fun, linked with a lively imagination, makes sex very attractive too. But remember not to tie them to your apron strings – they cannot survive that. Given just a little freedom, they make very good, interesting partners.

NARROWNESS

aimed for medicine when I u
and now wouldn't want that 'r
Then I considered forensic su
dismissed actor having complet
realized that I didn't want

The narrow writer tends to be timid, self-conscious and hypersensitive. Scared of making fools of themselves, such people feel anxious in social situations. They are more secure in fairly small spaces and in places they know well. Holidays tend to be predictable – the same place as last year! They like you to be by their side and may panic if left alone at a party or social gathering. Their insecurity and basic distrust of people can lead to embarrassing situations: in a group of people whom they don't know well, they may feel 'cornered' or 'got at'.

On the positive side, they are completely loyal to their partner, family and friends. They also have a highly developed sense of economy, collecting bits oi string, screws, nails, etc., in case these might come in useful one day. Make sure the right tools are always to hand as improvisation does not come easily to narrow writers. Sexually they exercise a lot of restraint.

12

Are You Tactful?

The *size of the letters at the ends of your words* will show how you rate with regard to this particular trait.

DECREASING

[handwritten: I am in Norway and. I am enjoying it]

A great deal of tact and diplomacy is shown here. You can safely introduce this writer to all your friends and family. He or she will also make you feel good about yourself by saying the right thing at the right moment. Nice to have around.

INCREASING

[handwritten: ...pears to my personality ...'d in my future career. year of a 4 year European ...alising in German) which ...s that I have as yet very]

Think carefully before taking this writer home to meet your mother. He or she is likely to blurt out the first thought that comes to mind and could cause offence. Have you ever been told, 'That outfit would look great if you lost some weight'? This is the type of person who would think nothing of saying it!

SOME OF EACH

I have just [written?] article in Over 21 magazine would be interested in [?] from my handwriting. I. handwriting and found.

Unpredictability is a problem. You can never be sure whether this writer will strike exactly the right note or cause you embarrassment. Interesting, but needs to be watched.

13

How Good Do You Feel About Yourself?

The *personal pronoun* 'I' shows how you feel about yourself and how you see yourself in relation to others.

19

SMALLER THAN REST OF SCRIPT
You don't value yourself enough.

I|

LARGER THAN REST OF SCRIPT
'Aren't I wonderful!' is the message you are shouting out to the world.

9|

SAME SIZE AS SCRIPT
No pretence here. You are the same in public as in private.

2

LIKE THE FIGURE 2
Sadly, you feel second-rate. Frequently produced by people who have a clever brother or sister.

1

SINGLE PLAIN STROKE
You are genuine and see yourself as you are.

I

PRINTED
You think clearly and have a high opinion of yourself.

i

LIKE A SMALL 'i'
You feel totally crushed and put down.

4

LIKE THE FIGURE 4
You cannot see anyone else's point of view.

g

AVERAGE-SIZE UPPER LOOP
You have a healthy self-respect.

g

NARROW UPPER LOOP
You are timid and well aware of it.

g

WIDE UPPER LOOP
You are over-emotional and have an exaggerated sense of your own importance.

d

ARC TO LEFT
Irresponsibility is shown here. Try sticking to your commitments.

d

HOOK TO LEFT
You can be greedy and unwilling to share.

TRIANGULAR BASE
Aggression can quickly surface.

CROSSED
Reveals strong fears and despondency.

DISCONNECTED STROKES
You are independent and love sporting activity.

SMALL WITH ADDITIONAL STROKES
You are uncertain of your own identity.

ANGULAR
You can be critical of yourself and hostile to others.

LARGE WITH ADDITIONAL FLOURISHES
A sign of vanity and vulgarity.

CURLED AND CLOSED
You have a self-protective and ungiving streak.

OPEN CIRCLE
You are looking for a mother figure.

LIKE A POUND SIGN
You see money as a source of personal value.

14

Do You Distance Yourself from Others?

—SPACING BETWEEN WORDS—

The space we leave between words shows the distance we like to maintain between ourselves and others.

VERY NARROW

People like this crave attention and can be quite selfish and insensitive to the needs of others. They are the types who butt in when you are having a private conversation with someone. If combined with very large handwriting, narrow spacing indicates generosity and even extravagance.

I fully realise that no job is perfect, but I still feel that somewhere there is a job that really suit me; that I can get excited about. The aspect of my present job that I like most is meeting the new clients

These are discriminating types. They afford others the privacy they need but, if invited to join in, will do so with a good grace and will behave in a pleasant manner. They show intelligence and inner organization.

VERY WIDE

I do admit to being moody I get quite down and at times and seem to

These writers need to maintain some distance and can experience difficulty in communicating. They feel very isolated at times.

FILLING IN ALL SPACE

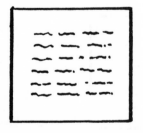

We all know people who write all around a card or letter, filling in every available bit of space. They are the ones who don't know when to stop talking or how to adapt their behaviour to suit the occasion. They say good-night half a dozen times on the doorstep and wake up all your neighbours at two o'clock in the morning, hooting their horn for good measure as they drive off. If you invite them, make sure you keep the whole day free!

──────── MARGINS ────────

Margins indicate the amount of space we need for ourselves.

BALANCED ALL ROUND

You don't put a foot wrong and treat all your family and friends with consideration and respect. You are a social asset, and also show good judgement.

WIDE ALL ROUND

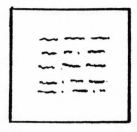

You can be aloof and uncertain about how to behave in social situations. You don't enjoy mixing and find it especially hard when you don't know people well.

WIDE LEFT

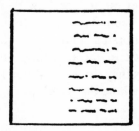

You are not too happy about the past but look to the future with a more positive attitude. Formality appeals to you; although you try hard to communicate well with others it does not come naturally.

WIDE RIGHT

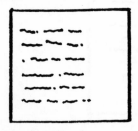

You are preoccupied with yourself at this moment and are wondering what the future holds in store for you. You find it difficult to face reality and are a poor mixer.

NARROWING LEFT

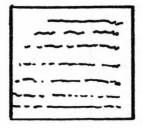

You are in the habit of making promises you know you can't fulfil. You also experience difficulty in moving forward and making decisions.

WIDENING LEFT

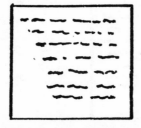

You are impatient, enthusiastic and expressive, and you find it hard to save money. You can become very absorbed in your interests and hobbies.

DEEP TOP

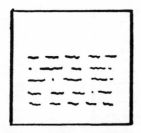

You like formality and show a great deal of respect for other people. You are also a caring person and you take the emotional and sexual needs of your partner into consideration.

SHALLOW TOP

Your needs always have to come first. You show a lack of consideration for others, with a tendency towards tactless and clumsy behaviour.

DEEP LOWER

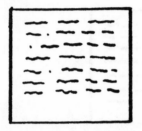

Your interest in other people quickly dissipates and you avoid commitment. You can be over-sensitive and take offence too quickly.

SHALLOW LOWER

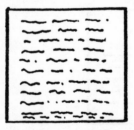

You have a tendency to become depressed. On some days you are completely uncommunicative, on others you are overbearing and no one else can get a word in. You lack self-discipline and are inclined to waste your energies.

NO MARGINS

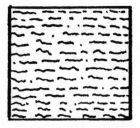

Anything goes when you are around – you rush in where angels fear to tread. Who says everyone finds you interesting? You can go right over the top, and you love spending money – but only on yourself!

UNEVEN

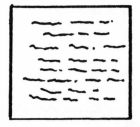

You are impulsive and a rebel, with a dislike of sensible rules and regulations. You invite strong positive and negative reactions from other people. Think before you speak! Rudeness comes easily to you.

15

How Do You Overcome Day-to-Day Obstacles?

The strength of your will-power and drive when coping with everyday challenges is shown by your *'t' crossings.*

SMALL
Shows timidity. You can't easily overcome problems as your will-power is weak.

BALANCED AND FIRM
You know what you want and use perfectly reasonable means to attain your goals.

LARGE
You go to any lengths to get what you want. Be careful you don't step on others in the process!

ABOVE DOWNSTROKE
You are quite unrealistic. Come down to earth!

TO THE RIGHT OF DOWNSTROKE
Slow down! You are in too much of a hurry and could overlook important details.

TO THE LEFT OF DOWNSTROKE
Your motto is, 'Don't do anything today that you can do tomorrow.'

NO CROSSING
By the time you get down to anything, you have forgotten what you wanted to do in the first place.

DOUBLE CROSSING
You show lack of confidence. You slow yourself down by checking and re-checking everything you do.

STRAIGHT AND RESTING ON TOP
You have high ideals and a strong will. You are also very protective towards family and friends.

VERY LOW
You feel inferior and always bow to the wishes of others.

ANGULAR
You are stubborn and determined, and you hate taking advice from anyone.

WAVY
You achieve a lot of what you set out to do, with the help of your lovely sense of humour.

CONCAVE
You are self-indulgent and tend to forget about the needs of others.

CONVEX
Shows discipline. You exercise a lot of control over your needs and drive.

CIRCULAR KNOT
You are a positive person and an achiever, but you act in a pleasant manner.

LOOPED STEM
You are quite vain and you try to attain your goals by using your charm.

FALLING
You give up easily and don't achieve a lot.

RISING
You are enthusiastic and try hard to achieve.

Note

Most of us will produce, say, two different crossings in the same piece of script, which is quite acceptable. Both interpretations will be valid. But a large variety of crossings does indicate some confusion between thoughts and actions.

16

Do You Have a Sense of Humour?

Seeing the funny side of life and not taking yourself too seriously can be of great help in overcoming difficulties together. Often when emotions reach boiling point, one or both partners will say or do something ridiculous that can change a tense atmosphere to one of laughter. But not everyone is secure enough to take such a self-detached view of themselves. When trying to spot a sense of humour in yourself or your partner, look for any stroke – or any letter of the alphabet – written in three directions (*three-way stroke*). These are some of the most common forms:

Shows a sense of fun and a talent for mimicry.

These writers laugh easily and look for the funny side of things.

F   K

These are our practical jokers.

Here we see our vulgar jokers – types who love telling dirty stories in the pub!

17

Are You Sexually Compatible?

The way we form the *loop on a 'g' or 'y'* is a good indication of our response in this important area of a relationship.

g

THE 'PERFECT LOVE LETTER'
A loving, warm person who is able to find contentment with one partner.

g y

ARCADED TO LEFT
Doesn't welcome responsibility in this area. If male, could run if you got pregnant.

g y

VERY NARROW LOOP
Finds difficulty in expressing sexual needs.

g y

VERY SHORT LOOP OR DOWNSTROKE
Little interest in sex, mainly because of lack of energy.

𝒢𝓎

SWINGING LEFTWARD MOVEMENT
A constant need for change and variety. Will try many different partners but is unlikely to be content with any one.

𝓆𝓎

STRAIGHT LEFTWARD STROKE
Enjoys self-gratification (masturbation).

𝓆 𝓎

CURLY DOWNSTROKE
An interesting partner. You need to be a bit of an athlete here – the missionary position will not satisfy this adventurous character.

𝓰 𝓳

VERY LOW ROUNDED LOOP
Hasn't yet found sexual satisfaction – an insensitive partner, perhaps?

𝓰

DOWNSTROKE WITH HEAVY PRESSURE, UPSTROKE WITH LIGHT PRESSURE
May start energetically but soon falls asleep at your side. If male, the type who boasts about the good time he can give you in bed.

DOWNSTROKE WITH LIGHT PRESSURE, UPSTROKE WITH HEAVY PRESSURE

They take a long time to get going but will surprise you with their agility and sexual adventurousness.

HOURGLASS FORMATION ON LOWER LOOP

People who handle other people's bodies – nurses, doctors, etc. – produce this particular movement. Suggests a clinical approach.

EXAGGERATED AND UNUSUAL MOVEMENTS

Often found in the handwriting of individuals with lesbian or homosexual tendencies, either active or latent.

BREAK IN UPSTROKE

Most commonly found in men who have had a vasectomy or women with gynaecological problems.

HOOKED ENDING ON UPSTROKE

These people are so concerned about their own enjoyment that they forget you are participating.

q y

SMALL ANGLE
Tyrannical nature due to sexual frustration.

q y

LARGE ANGLE
Really aggressive due to sexual frustration.

q y

REVERSED ENDING
Sublimates sexual urges by doing good works.

g y

HEAVY PRESSURE WITH INFLATED LOWER LOOP
Strong sexual appetite. Three times a day, and isn't going to let up!

q y

STRAIGHT DOWNSTROKE
Will instigate sex only when they feel like it. A selfish partner.

UPSTROKE STOPS SHORT
Enjoys the chase and the flirting but fears penetration.

ANGLED AND LOOPED DOWNSTROKE
The type who always leaves the light on and loves to look at their own and their partner's naked body. Sexually vain.

TICK ON DOWNSTROKE
A very nervous partner who needs a lot of encouragement and reassurance.

Note

A writer who always produces his or her 'g' and 'y' in the same way shows little imagination in the sexual act. Half a dozen different types of loop show someone who is easily turned on and has some lack of control. The average person produces two to three different loop (or straight-stroke) formations, indicating a healthy, imaginative interest in sex.

18

Signatures: Your Personal Thumb-Print

Your *signature* shows how you would like other people to see you.

Same Size
Anne Jones

LEGIBLE, SAME SIZE AS SCRIPT
You behave the same in public as in private. A genuine person.

Please do this
as quickly as
possible.

Elaine D'Angelo

LARGE IN RELATION TO REST OF SCRIPT
You seek recognition and could be hiding a feeling of inferiority.

FIRM UNDERLINE
You have a good degree of confidence.

DOUBLE UNDERLINE
You are putting yourself above others.

SMALL IN RELATION TO REST OF SCRIPT
You make a pretence of modesty.

SMALL UNDERLINE AT END
You would like to have the last word but doubt whether you'll get away with it.

LINE ABOVE AND BELOW
You are self-protective and do not trust others.

LINE THROUGH LOWER-CASE LETTERS
Your self-esteem is low and you have a poor self-image.

ENCLOSED IN A CIRCLE
You try to hide your true intentions.

'T' CROSSING EXTENDED OVER REST OF LETTERS
You are very protective towards family and friends.

RISING
You are professionally ambitious.

FALLING
You may have been depressed or tired at the time of writing.

H.S. TAN

T. M. Mc DONALD

ILLEGIBLE
You are secretive and lack consideration. However, if you are in the habit of signing a lot of letters every day, it could merely suggest that you have a quick mind.

FULL STOP AFTER
You always want the last word.

TWO FULL STOPS AFTER
You always insist that you are right.

WAVY UNDERLINE
You have a nice sense of humour and you don't take yourself
too seriously.

UNNECESSARY ADDITION TO FIRST STROKE
You have a habit of putting obstacles in other people's way.

UNNECESSARY ADDITION TO LAST STROKE
You don't know when to stop talking about yourself.

VERY ELABORATE UNDERLINING
You tend to be over-familiar – someone who immediately
gets on to first-name terms.

J.M. Sprake

USE OF INITIALS ONLY
You are cautious – or formal in appropriate circumstances.

Catriona Marshall.

USE OF FULL NAME
You are a friendly person who likes to put others at their ease.

CHRISTIAN NAME AND SURNAME JOINED
You aim to make the maximum use of your personality.

SURNAME LARGER
You have a lot of respect for your husband or father.

David Smallwood

SURNAME SMALLER
If you are a woman, you appear to be unhappy with your partner; if a man, you don't feel much respect for your father.

Simon T. Bates

SMALL MIDDLE INITIAL
You dislike that particular name.

How They Write

Secrets of the Famous
Revealed by a Leading Graphologist

For Fred, Edward, Frank and Marie

INTRODUCTION

When we first learn to write we conform to a specific style referred to by graphologists as 'copybook'. This obviously varies from country to country but, providing a graphologist has copies of the various styles taught throughout the world, it should not present a problem. It is the deviation from the original style that sets the graphologist on a wonderful voyage of discovery. All the interpretations are based on an established body of knowledge but much depends on the skill of the particular graphologist in arriving at an interpretation and conveying it in a language that is clearly understood.

Graphology can reveal the writer's individuality, originality, leadership qualities, motivation, intelligence, tastes and interests, ability to overcome day-to-day obstacles, and very much more. The dominant movements in handwriting that lead us to our interpretations are the size, slant, speed, pressure, forms of connection, angularity, roundness, broadness, narrowness, layout, spacing and, to a lesser extent, the individual letter forms. The personal pronoun 'I' plays its own particular part, as do the 'i' dots and 't' crosses.

Many of you will say, 'I never write the same way twice!' The dominants change little but mood changes which result in a slightly different appearance to the layman are easily detected by the trained eye of the graphologist. There are times when one sees a great deterioration in the handwriting movements and these are readily recognised as periods of great stress, bereavement or illness. Character traits that deviate from the considered norm will instantly show up in the handwriting.

Graphology is used widely not only by individuals wishing to gain greater insight into their own personality but also by companies wishing to employ the most suitable applicants. It is also used in vocational and marriage guidance, in education and in crime detection. It is practised throughout Europe and the United

States, where it is an established academic subject taught in universities. It does, however, have its limitations. Age, for example, cannot be judged with total accuracy. A person's actual age is often at variance with his mental age. How often have we heard the remark, 'That child was born old' or, 'Will he/she ever grow up?' The sex of a person can also present problems. Men may have feminine traits and women may have masculine ones. What is certain is that we are all a mixture of both. Since age and sex have a bearing on character analysis, it is always wise to establish these from the outset. Handwriting can tell you nothing about the future but it can indicate the writer's potential and enable you to give an estimate of his future performance.

Like a fingerprint, every person's handwriting is unique to them. Most of us will recognise the handwriting of our friends and relatives on envelopes as they drop through the letter box. The famous people in this book have all left, or are leaving, their mark in the world and the most dominant and interesting factor to be found in their handwriting is that they all possess a mixture of positive and negative traits. They are just like you and I.

My special thanks to those many people who, during my twelve years of cruising around the world lecturing on graphology, have provided me with the samples and the opportunity to analyse the handwriting of the rich and famous.

Gloria Hargreaves

SCIENCE AND THE ARTS

Maria Callas
Opera Singer

This lady had one way of working and one way only – she showed consistency, a systematic approach to everything she undertook and the desire to complete any task in a logical manner. All of this is seen in the total connectedness of the script. She had a great dislike of interruption until she felt she had come to a proper stopping point. The whole shows dedication, steadfastness and an explosive nature confirmed by the erratic pressure.

Sir Colin Davis
Conductor

The very thick stroke of the creative artist. Angular movements show a lot of mental energy and the comma 'i' dot shows curiosity and observation. The script is totally connected, revealing the writer to be very logical and quite compulsive. He is restless and needs stimulation to avoid boredom. A challenge has great appeal to him. He is an extremely mature and intelligent individual. The final 's' shows originality in thought and action, and the rising signature indicates professional ambition.

Jerome Kern
Composer

This totally disconnected script falls into a very creative category. This is the writing of an inspired individualist who personally was egocentric, somewhat insecure and rather moody. He was also intuitive and very much open to the influences of the moment. He was super-sensitive, as shown by the extremely light pressure, and took offence easily. He could be stubborn and uncooperative. His signature, which is larger than the script, suggests that he presented a far more extroverted personality than was indeed the fact.

Wolfgang Amadeus Mozart
Composer

A signature that looks as if it has been executed with a paint-brush. This intensely passionate individual became totally

absorbed in anything he undertook. He was extremely hot-blooded and sensual. He delighted in nature and all it had to offer. The sickle-like shape at the bottom of the 'z' shows a certain sadistic streak and the whole shows undisciplined daydreaming and sexual fantasy.

Sergei Vassilievich Rachmaninoff
Composer and pianist

This totally disconnected handwriting speaks of the writer's wealth of creative and original ideas which continually inspired and filled his mind. An extraordinarily intuitive individual, who had the ability to make decisions instantly, he was endowed with an unusual imagination and was given to meditation, dreams and premonitions. He was witty, had great presence of mind, and could well have succeeded in the literary world. Poetry was one of his great loves. He was prone to spells of moodiness, outbursts of temper, and tantrums. He had a tendency to break off social relationships for no apparent reason. He loved beauty in all its shapes and forms.

Dame Joan Sutherland
Opera singer

A lady who tries to maintain an optimistic front at all times but does not always succeed, as shown by the bowed base to her signature. The writing is quite rounded, indicating a kindly, pleasant nature, and the full loops suggest emotional outbursts. She is sometimes secretive (note the closed 'o's and 'a's) and communicates best with those known well to her. The pull of the final 'd', used as an underline, hints at her pride in previous successes rather than looking to the future with confidence.

Thomas Alva Edison
Inventor

This fascinating, extremely squared writing tells of a materialistic individual who liked possessions for the sense of security they brought him. It also shows that he was logical, practical and thoroughly enjoyed working with his hands. He was independent and had difficulty in relating his thoughts and ideas to other people. His very accurately placed 'i' dots speak of his obsession with detail, whilst those elongated 't' crosses reveal his great will power and ability to overcome any obstacle. A man who would not let up. A cold personality but a brilliant mind.

Albert Einstein
Physicist and mathematician

This very tiny handwriting tells us of an introverted, shy and reserved individual who had no wish to appear in the limelight. He could work for hours alone on a project and his powers of concentration were tremendous. Every 'i' is dotted, every 't' is crossed with great precision, showing his concern for accuracy in all things. The evenness of the word and line spacing shows his absolute clarity of thought and painstaking desire to be thorough and consistent. He was receptive to ideas from other people (indicated by the breadth of the writing) but was basically a loner who felt overrated when given any praise. The extremely large 't' crossing in 'Einstein' suggests a protective attitude towards others.

Sir Alexander Fleming
Discoverer of penicillin

The small handwriting that denotes the scientific mind. These are the thinkers of the world rather than the doers. The

I have no use for them

Alexander Fleming

writer could concentrate for long periods of time on a project, as seen by the complete connectedness of the letters. The small personal pronoun 'I' indicates he was a very modest man, but the slightly larger signature suggests that he liked to appear more confident. The unusual little hooked starting stroke on the 'h' shows how he held on to ideas and didn't give up easily, while the 'i' dot to the far right reveals both impatience and curiosity. The curl on the capital 'F' shows he was proud of his achievements.

Sigmund Freud
Originator of psychoanalysis

A man of high ideals, as shown by the tall upper loops, who was frequently disappointed in his fellow humans. (Note the falling words at the ends of lines.) At times he became quite melancholy. He was basically introverted and compulsive in his behavioural patterns. It is an angular script, showing mental energy. This was someone who did not often change his ideas. The upward-pointing strokes reveal his desire for recognition and achievement on a mental level, but resentment towards past events in his life is also in evidence. Some breaks between letters indicate intuition and perception, whilst his sharp strokes show he could size up situations easily and had a quick grasp of facts. He experienced difficulty in relating intimately to his own sex.

Jeffrey Archer
Popular-fiction writer

The rather gate-like construction of the signature tells us of a man who puts up barriers and obstacles. He dislikes anyone prying into his moods or motives. This is both an analytical and a calculating script. Because of the variation in the letter sizes at the ends of words, we see someone who can change from discretion to complete tactlessness. The 'n' in 'reading' shows his enquiring mentality, whilst the simplicity of the letter formations tells of his direct approach to solving problems. The swinging, large movements in the lower zone indicate a need for change and variety in his sex life. He is also quite materialistic.

Robert Browning
Poet

[handwritten text]

The light pressure and sharp writing show a sensitive individual who was critical both of himself and others. He was quite obsessive about cleanliness and had a cold, remote manner. Spiritual and idealistic, he was disappointed with his fellow humans and felt in many ways that he did not fit in. He was not gifted with a high energy level but saved what energy he had until it was needed. He could have a sharp tongue, as shown by the small, pointed 't' crosses. A man who took offence very easily.

Barbara Cartland
Romantic novelist

[handwritten text]

The enormous signature clearly shows the writer's love of recognition and of being in the public eye. Underneath, however, is a very private person who enjoys time alone and who is capable of working for long periods alone on a project, as confirmed by the small middle-zone letters. She is logical, works steadily and dislikes interruptions en route. She is idealistic (tall upper-zone letters) and is frequently disappointed that others do not share the high standards she expects of herself. She likes food, as shown by the open top on the 'g' in 'good'. Despite her success the very large spaces between the words indicate feelings of isolation and of being out of step with the rest of the world. (*Shown slightly reduced.*)

Agatha Christie
Detective-story writer

A very clearly written signature with many breaks between letters, showing a lot of intuition. The opening at the top of the 'A' indicates quite a talkative nature and someone who was open to new experiences or ideas. The writer was a very likeable lady with lots of imagination, as seen in the fullness of the letters. She was broad-minded and uninhibited. A generous nature is revealed, as is a degree of quiet confidence, shown by the small underline. A charming, delightful person who was honest, frank and direct.

Charles Dickens
Novelist

The ornate 'C' hints at vulgarity and ostentation, which is confirmed by the excessive underlining of the name. The 'i' in 'Dickens', written like an 'e', suggests pseudo charm, and the large middle-zone letters suggest a rather self-centred individual who made great issue of trivial matters. He worked well in a systematic manner but he was difficult to get along with. He placed great emphasis on personal appearance and was quite highly sexed with a very visual mind.

F. Scott Fitzgerald
Novelist

A rather artistic signature showing creativity and imagination. From its large size we can see that the writer liked being involved in large-scale projects and had ambition and a high energy level. He had a desire, too, for tactile stimulation and a need for physical closeness with others. A deep capacity for the enjoyment of new experiences is also in evidence. The script is quite disconnected, which suggests he used a lot of intuition in his projects. The strokes are firm and indicate both self-assurance and a good sense of timing. A positive individual who could at times be very adamant. Warm natured but somewhat repressed sexually.

W. Somerset Maugham
Writer

little white folds.
clean and for a
tired wings.

W. Somerset Maugham

A tactful individual, as seen by the decreasing letters at the ends of the words. The slight slant to the right shows the writer's desire to communicate his feelings and ideas to others, and the 'i' dots, again always to the right, show how impatient and frustrated he could be as his thoughts came to him quicker than he could write them down. It's a connected script, revealing him to be logical and able to work for long periods at a time alone on a project. In fact, he strongly disliked interruptions. The very consistent word and line spacing indicate a man who was organised and planned his time well and effectively. Some lovely connecting strokes between the words 'white' and 'folds' tell us of his original thinking. This is the writing of an uncomplicated individual who thoroughly enjoyed using his mental talents to the full.

John Mortimer
Novelist and playwright

This writer is very intelligent with a great deal of mental energy, as revealed by the angular movements. Firmness, inflexibility and determination are all confirmed by the heavy pressure. This is the handwriting of a blunt-spoken individual who hates to have his moods or motives questioned. A lot of pride and a strong ego are shown in the largeness of the signature, and the 'p' in 'up' indicates stubbornness.

George Bernard Shaw
Dramatist and critic

This small script reveals a man of considerable ability, one who did not seek approval for his words or actions and had good powers of concentration. Some of the letters are ink-filled, showing he could be explosive, and the long hook at the end of 'Shaw' indicates that he held very firmly to his ideas and possessions. It is a narrow script, suggesting that he was tense and somewhat sceptical. Any wastage of time or materials irritated him. He was gifted at solving abstract problems but had little understanding of the emotions of those close to him. A man who was fond of studying and reading till the end of his days. (*Signature shown enlarged.*)

Oscar Wilde
Writer and wit

Oscar Wilde (signature)

A very broad, simplified script without any superfluous strokes whatsoever. A great freedom lover who had little desire for personal possessions, this writer needed space, travel, large rooms in which to spread himself, and had a ready acceptance of new ideas and experiences. He was tolerant and accepted others for what they were. His energy level was not high but he paced himself well in order to prolong his staying power. His ideas were very personal and often quite inventive. There is no hint of aggression or anger in his writing. His motto in life was 'live and let live'.

Salvador Dali
Artist

i am walking down the street / to get the / horse and carriage / out of the old garage (handwritten note and signature)

A very difficult personality and one given to many changes of mood, as indicated by the variable letter sizes. He was both inspired and rebellious. He liked behaving in an unacceptable manner and delighted in shocking people. He was gifted and original in his thinking, but day-to-day responsibilities remained a mystery to him. He could be very sarcastic (sharp letter formations), persistent (knotted 't's) and tactless in the extreme. A creative individual who worked in fits and starts.

His emotional nature was erratic and he was completely undisciplined. The large signature tells us he was in love with himself but had little understanding of what made him tick!

Henry Moore
Sculptor

Henry Moore

The angularity of this signature tells of a keen, agile mind, and the roundness of the 'o's in 'Moore' reveals kindness towards his fellow humans. Yet the whole suggests a demanding nature – one that was not easily satisfied. This writer was a great striver and rarely pleased with his efforts. The last, falling stroke on the 'e' suggests he felt disappointed with some of his past relationships. A very intelligent and mature individual, he could at times be quite morose.

Pablo Picasso
Artist

Picasso

A simple and aesthetic signature reveals clear, if unusual, thinking processes. This was a man who disliked clutter. His great imagination is shown in the very large 'P', and its irregular formation indicates a certain rebelliousness. He behaved without face or façade and didn't really care whether other people liked him or not. He had tremendous intuition and relied totally upon it. A poetic individual.

Walt Disney
Film producer and cartoonist

An imaginative and emotional individual, as shown by the large loops and capital letters. There is a great deal of originality to every movement of the writing, clearly indicating an innovative and creative person who delighted in his talent. The pressure shows warmth and a sense of fun. The loops on the 'n' show he could be charming even to those he did not like, but the knotted 'a' is a sign of secretiveness – he would convey his ideas to others only when he chose to. The whole reveals his love of fun, a sense of humour and a great intensity of feeling.

Sir Alfred Hitchcock
Film director

A very speedy, quick-flowing script showing an agile mind and rapidity of thought. All the letters are linked together, revealing great powers of concentration. The writer did everything according to his own ideas and was not bound in any way by convention. He was exacting, persistent and always carried his plans through to the end. The connectedness of the words and the large lower loops show how he delighted in exercising his power of artistic expression. He also had a well-developed appreciation of music. An impulsive man who sometimes squandered his wealth unnecessarily. His sex drive was also quite powerful and tact was not his strong point.

Florence Nightingale
'The Lady with the Lamp'

A kindly person who pushed herself to the limit. The left-slanting downward stroke on the 'y' shows this writer sub-limated her sex drive in the service of others, but she was also very progressive, as seen by the pull of the writing to the right. Tomorrow was all-important to her. She liked people and liked to communicate with them, was proud, idealistic and very demonstrative. She could be impulsive, overtaxed herself and, at times, suffered periods of exhaustion. The funny curl on the 'F' in 'Florence' shows her reaching up for inspiration and suggests a sense of humour, too. She was a brave lady but not always practical and rather inclined to overreact. She did not always absorb or learn from past experiences.

John Young
Astronaut

The leanness of the writer's strokes tells of his technical training, while the loop on 'John' shows his thoroughness. The rising signature confirms his professional ambition. Note that the first stroke on 'John' is amazingly like the nose cone of an aircraft, done completely subconsciously! The full lower loops show a very high energy level and strong materialistic and sexual interests. The connectedness of the script indicates his logical approach to life and his ability to work in a very systematic manner. His powers of concentration are excellent.

POLITICS

James Callaghan
Prime Minister (1976–1979)

Well begun is half
done ! – As so they used to say.
Anyway congratulations
on what you have managed so far.

Jim Callaghan

The fairly light pressure of this script shows that the writer is
not gifted naturally with an abundance of energy. However
the general regularity of the handwriting suggests consistency of effort, and the quick movement across the page indicates speedy and agile mental processes. The absence of
angular letter forms shows his desire to settle problems by
conciliatory means. A dislike of noise and aggression is also
in evidence. The baseline is a little too flexible: he may allow
himself to be influenced too much by other people. His letters

are a mixture of broadness, revealing courage and directness, and narrowness, showing caution and restraint. One feels he could have achieved a lot more in his lifetime. His signature says that he conducts himself the same in public as in private.

Sir Winston Churchill
Prime Minister (1940–1945; 1951–1955)

Know, according to the ... in your department. dates on which all Dreadnoughts ... built have been (a) order (c) launched (d) ...

A very simplified handwriting showing a high degree of intellectual discipline. The writer's skill as a leader is seen in his foresight (letters moving clearly to the right), orderliness and quick grasp of essentials. The sharp 't' crosses tell of his strong will and directness. The regular, even strokes show his ability to concentrate, plus a sense of order and punctuality. He was industrious, persevering and conscientious. The excellent word and line spacing clearly indicate his great planning and organising ability. He was a good decision maker and was indifferent to what others thought about him.

Edward Heath
Prime Minister (1970–1974)

The simplicity of the strokes indicates efficiency and a desire for truth and accuracy. This person keeps his emotions under control and is direct in his manner of speaking. The script is quite broad and shows his expansiveness in social situations; however he is always on his guard and can appear formal and cold. His musical talent is revealed by the first stroke of the 'H' in 'Heath'. The large capitals show a lot of pride and the underlining denotes self-assurance, although the small letters hint at a certain reserve. He is a quietly confident man who tends to stand back and watch rather than push himself to the forefront.

Michael Heseltine
Conservative politician

A totally disconnected script, showing that this writer's opinions are based on instinct rather than logic. He has a brilliant and original mind and great literary talents. He can grasp essentials instantly and act upon them. He is very critical of himself and others and is particularly sensitive, often taking offence when none is intended. He is egocentric, moody and restless. The very wide spacing between his words indicates feelings of isolation; he can even feel lonely in a crowded room. He fears contact and closeness with

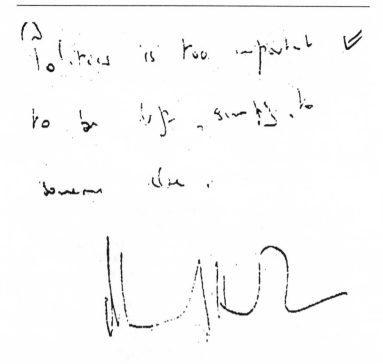

others. From the large spaces between the lines it can be seen that he has difficulty in trusting his fellow men. However, he holds himself in high esteem. His illegible signature confirms all of the above.

Douglas Hurd
Conservative politician

A direct, honest, likeable and articulate person who nevertheless plays his cards close to his chest. This is shown by the rounded base to his letters and the angular tops. The reversed 'd' tells us he is very self-protective and quick to defend himself and his opinions. The whole shows him as hard-working, loyal and sincere. Reliability is seen in the even baseline, and literary ability in the breaks between letters. Charm runs throughout: a soft exterior but quite tough underneath.

Neil Kinnock
Leader of the Labour party

A speedy script which shows a quick-thinking individual with a high degree of mental and physical energy. The sharp points on the 'm's reveal a critical and investigative mind which explores and digs for knowledge, always asking questions and seeking answers. He is impetuous in his expression of emotion, as seen by the frequent connection of his letters. He is thorough, systematic and persistent, and aims to see things through to a successful conclusion – even, at times, to the bitter end. However, he can get bogged down with detail and can miss the overall meaning. His firm, long 't' crosses show his protectiveness towards his family and colleagues alike. Job satisfaction is more important to him than material gain. There is little energy left over for sexual pursuits (small endstrokes on 'y's) but otherwise he makes a kindly, affectionate partner.

John Major
Prime Minister (1990–)

The very tall upper-zone letters tell us that this is a man of intelligence and ambition, but because it is a narrow script we

John Major

know he is never satisfied with his own achievements. He always feels the need to prove himself and has a demanding conscience and uncompromising ideas of right and wrong. The small middle-zone letters indicate someone of great independence who does not seek the approval of others and who is not particularly concerned about his popularity. Firm downstrokes show a good sense of timing and the whole suggests that he is economical and has a dislike of wastefulness. He is a loyal, honest and reliable man with a dry sense of humour. Great responsibility could take its toll on his health, as he becomes tense and nervous under pressure but will never show it. (*Shown slightly reduced.*)

Sir Denis Thatcher
Businessman; husband of Margaret Thatcher

Indeed says anything for publication, "I is ... Denis Thatcher

Margaret chose well when she picked Denis as her partner. The good pressure tells us that he is a warm, affectionate and supportive husband. He can also be very stubborn and follow his own interests and hobbies no matter who objects! He is a lover of nature and kindly to people less fortunate than himself. He has a generosity of spirit and considerable charm. This is very positive handwriting indicating business acumen, and the strong 'p' shows how he follows his ideas through. Some of the ovals are slightly ink-filled, so he likes a tipple and good food. He has a colourful imagination and, on occasions, is prone to explosive outbursts, but he is warm-natured and sublimates some of his sexual energy in good deeds. His signature shows materialism.

Margaret Thatcher
Prime Minister (1979–1990)

A very quick script showing speed of thought, energy and progressive thinking. The simplification of the letter formations indicates the writer's direct approach and a desire to simplify issues. She loathes waffle of any type and has a great capacity for the quick grasp, comprehension and assimilation of essentials. A combination of connected and disconnected strokes shows she is capable of a happy mixture of imagination and intelligence to put her vision into effect and make her dreams come true. Negatively, she is very intolerant of those who disagree with her and does not make a good listener. Her signature reveals her to be genuine; she believes in every word she utters. Sexually, she is always in a hurry, needs little sleep and has a clinical approach to this area of her life. She probably enjoys playing the piano just as much!

Sir Harold Wilson
(Baron Wilson of Rievaulx)
Prime Minister (1964–1970; 1974–1976)

LONDON, SW1

They tried to tell us we're too young. But they were wrong, weren't they? Best wishes, Harold Wilson.

The smallness here tells of this writer's capacity for accuracy and his aptitude for detailed and scientific work. His powers of concentration are excellent, plus he has an extremely retentive memory. He is a thinker rather than a doer, a particularly clever individual who could be somewhat manipulative. Despite his shyness and reserve, bordering on an inferiority complex, he has quite a power drive. A man of great ability who appears to have been held back by a lack of self-confidence. The ink-filled ovals suggest he can be explosive at times and has a liking for a tipple!

31

George Bush
President of the United States (1989–)

[handwritten text]

— for them, but
I hope I have
ed shape them
sent. Sincerely,
Cg Bush

This script shows a man with a quick, alert mind, but because of the uneven baseline it also indicates that he can become excitable and, at times, moody. He is very versatile, impatient and progressive. The pointed tops on the 'm' and 'n' reveal his penetrating intelligence and his ability to simplify issues and come to rapid conclusions. The majority of his 'o's and 'a's are closed, showing discretion, and diplomacy and tact are strongly indicated by the decrease in the size of the letters at the ends of words. He does not possess a high energy level so has to take care to pace himself well. The printed 'I', in an otherwise cursive script, speaks of great independence and clear original thinking. Ball games appeal to him.

Jimmy Carter
President of the United States (1977–1981)

The many breaks between the letters here reveal a man whose judgements are based on intuition. He has the ability to size up situations quickly and is very observant. The rising lines are a sign of enthusiasm, but the script is a little too right-slanting, which indicates strong emotional reactions and impulsiveness. Some memory lapses are shown by the unexplained large gaps between letters. It is a fast script suggesting a quick mind and directness. A progressive, *[handwritten note]* The beautiful book & lighter will always remind me of your hospitality —

[signature] Jimmy

inspired individual who experiences difficulty in controlling his emotional reactions. He is quick to take offence and often feels restless and unsettled.

Edward Kennedy
Democrat politician

[signature: Edward M Kennedy]

The pressure here is very variable, indicating moodiness and erratic working patterns, but the simplicity of the strokes reveals efficiency and the ability to recognise essentials. When the writer applies himself, therefore, he works extremely well; at other times, he seems disinterested. The small middle-zone letters speak of difficulty in delegating and of lack of trust in others. The abrupt finish on the 'd' in 'Edward' tells of disappointments in personal relationships. The signature falls and rises, indicating that he wishes to appear enthusiastic but does not always succeed. The X-like 'y' in the surname, which is also found in Robert Kennedy's signature, suggests a fear of death.

Jacqueline (Kennedy) Onassis
First Lady of the United States (1961–1963)

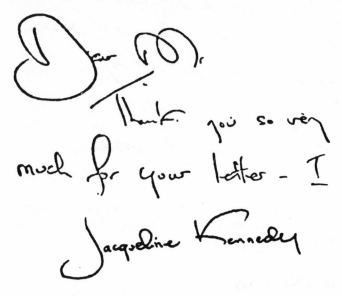

The simple strokes show great intelligence and their height speaks of an idealistic lady with a strong spiritual leaning. It is a slightly left-slanting script, revealing sensitivity but also indicating a person who can be charming outwardly whilst inwardly remaining aloof. The very small middle-zone letters tell of her creative ability but also reveal that she was not content on a day-to-day basis. The large 'k' in 'Thank' speaks of some rebelliousness. There are a lot of disconnected letters that reveal great intuition and the ability to size up situations very quickly. Negatively, the 'K' in 'Kennedy' tells of a condescending attitude.

John F. Kennedy
President of the United States (1961–1963)

The speed of the writing indicates an extremely quick-thinking and agile mind. The letters decrease in size at the ends of words, showing tact, diplomacy and manipulative qualities. This thready type of writing is identified with very high intelligence, broad vision and original ideas, but the 't' crossings vary in length revealing unpredictability. An impatient individual who drove himself and others hard, and had a high energy level and sex drive.

Robert F. Kennedy
Democrat statesman

This hastily written script reveals an alert, speedy mind and a high energy level. The firm downstrokes show the enthusiasm the writer brought to anything he became interested in. He had a warm, sensual nature but could be sarcastic and cutting in his remarks. The thickness of the downstrokes shows he was very self-centred and had a quick

[handwritten note: in my candidacy please don't answer this publicly, with signature]

temper. He also had a great deal of energy for sporting and sexual pursuits. The writing is narrow, indicating that he frequently felt inhibited and restrained, which in turn made him frustrated and angry. The X-like 'y' in 'Kennedy' clearly shows fear of death and confirms that he was disappointed in his achievements.

Martin Luther King
American civil-rights leader

[handwritten signature: Martin Luther King Jr.]

This right-slanting script shows an individual who looked to the future, but the starting stroke on the 'M' and the hook on the 't' cross tell us that he took many ideas from the past along with him. Leadership qualities and idealism are shown by the size, and the loops reveal great emotion. He could laugh and cry easily and readily gave vent to his feelings. This man overreacted to situations and had quite a power complex. Energetic and stubborn, he held firmly to his ideas. He needed recognition and acted with boldness and optimism. Negatively he could be boastful and dogmatic.

Abraham Lincoln
President of the United States (1860–1865)

Extremely balanced writing which shows good, sound judgement. It is also very connected, indicating the writer's progressive and logical ideas. He worked well, systematically and with great concentration and attention to detail. His letters are firm, showing a good sense of timing, and the evenness of the baseline speaks of reliability and emotional stability. Not the most inspired man but a man of integrity, honesty and directness. He believed in everything he said; he was a good decision maker and was discreet and caring in his use of words. There is only one sign of rebelliousness and that is in the split 'k' in 'know'. A very trustworthy, honest man, who suffered with some pain in his fingers.

Richard Nixon
President of the United States (1969–1974)

The first signature, taken from early in the writer's career, shows a very logical individual, someone who had a clear goal in sight and was persistent. He was also well-balanced, honest, reliable and dedicated to every task in hand. His mind was filled with curiosity, and his desire to lead was great, as shown by the large capitals and the connectedness. His loops show he was emotionally healthy and quick-thinking.

By the time he left office, his signature had disintegrated to an illegible line; he obviously felt he had lost control. He was still clinging on desperately, as seen by the hooked 'i' dot. He was also experiencing difficulty in communicating with those around him and could not be pinned down to a particular course of action.

Ronald Reagan
President of the United States (1981–1989)

The great simplicity of the capitals indicates the writer's pride and ambition; their largeness is the sign of a showman. The gap after the first 'R' reveals his power of observation, and the slightly old-fashioned style his respect for tradition. The connectedness tells us that he is objective and purposeful in his attitudes. The whole suggests an ordinary 'Mr Nice Guy', who is idealistic but often suspicious of the moods and

Well Here's everything

Ronald Reagan

motives of those around him. He does not have a great imagination and the very high 't' cross reveals that some of his ideas are not based on practicality!

Fidel Castro
Prime Minister of Cuba (1959–)

Fidel Castro

A flamboyant, attention-seeking individual is shown here. He is very domineering, as seen by the large, extended top on the 'F' in 'Fidel'. The hard angles reveal someone who greatly dislikes interference of any type. The heavy pressure shows a high energy level, a strong will and a forceful personality. A very proud, self-opinionated man who can, just occasionally, show some softness. This is indicated by the rounded capital 'C' in 'Castro'. He uses harshness and forcefulness to dominate and control others. A very strong personality whose desire is to leave his mark on the environment.

Oliver Cromwell
Lord Protector (1653–1658)

This large, angular script speaks of the writer's leadership qualities, mental energy and self-righteousness. The angularity also reveals that the complexity of human emotion baffled him and any appeal made to him had to be based on logic. He thrived on facts. He was both compulsive and a perfectionist. His pen never left the paper during the penning of this signature, revealing his stubbornness and his desire always to have the last word. He expected others to follow him without question, but the varying pressure tells of erratic outbursts and a lack of consistency in decision making. His ego was huge.

Mahatma Gandhi
Indian political and spiritual leader

A kindly, strong individual who needed to be with people, as shown by the closeness of the personal pronoun 'I' to the word 'am'. Innovative thinking is indicated by the connections between the words 'to', 'send' and 'you'. There is both rebelliousness and humility in the script. The broadness tells of his great courage and also of his need for space. The 'p' in 'copies' hints at stubbornness. His powers of concentration were excellent and his approach to problem solving very original. A particularly gifted man, whose rising signature reveals his ambition and humour. The wavy underlining suggests that he needed to have the last word but did not always expect to be taken seriously.

Charles de Gaulle
President of France (1959–1969)

The smallness of the script indicates great powers of concentration and very good attention to detail. At times this writer was impatient, and the heavy final full stop at the end of his signature tells us that he liked to have the last word. He was in many respects a reserved individual who welcomed time alone. The speed of the writing indicates his ability to think, act and move quickly. He could be intolerant of those less well informed than himself, and his signature, slightly larger than the script, shows he could behave in a superior manner. Its rising slant also shows his professional ambition. This is the writing of a very clever individual who would have risen to the top in any profession he had chosen.

Heinrich Himmler
Head of the German SS and the Gestapo (1936–1945)

A very aggressive signature showing great inflexibility, determination and rigidity. A man who could not be argued with; his word was law. He had the desire to impose his will

on others and harboured feelings of resentment towards
society. Considerable energy and vigour is in evidence. He
had an aptitude for hard work and thoroughness and
enjoyed surmounting obstacles and solving difficult problems. A love of order is shown, as is his ability to plan ahead.
A hard, austere man who had a dislike of ease and comfort
and was baffled by human emotion. The club-shaped crossing on the first initial shows hostility and aggression.

Adolf Hitler
German Führer (1934–1945)

At the time this signature was written, the writer was trying
to maintain an optimistic front, as shown by the arcade shape
of the signature, but he was not succeeding. The ink-filled
ovals speak of an explosive temperament and one given to
excesses in all areas. The letters are very narrow, showing
him to be tense, uptight and intolerant. The very involved
capital 'H' is a sign of coarseness and vulgarity, and the high
't' cross shows high ideals and sarcasm. The whole suggests
an angry, self-doubting and depressed frame of mind.

Karl Marx
Founder of modern Communism

The very small handwriting of the exacting personality who is
a perfectionist in everything he does. This writer welcomed
the chance to work alone for long periods of time and was
happiest when unobserved. He had an academic mentality

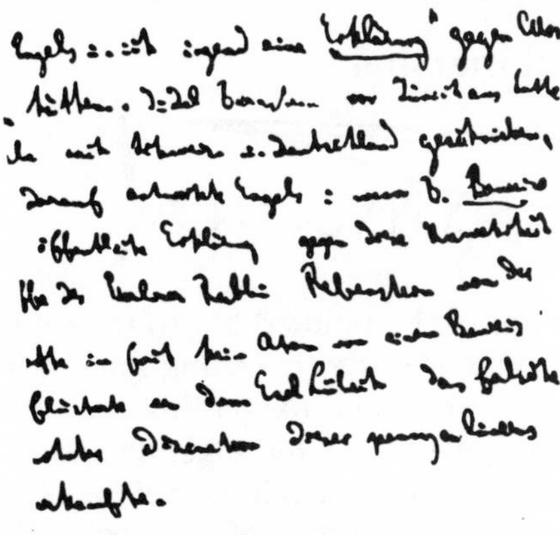

and was unconcerned about what others thought of him. He was very persistent (some knotted letters), pedantic and, on occasions, uptight and explosive. Some leftward movements show he was strongly influenced by the past. He experienced difficulty in relating intimately in close relationships.

Napoleon I (Napoleon Bonaparte)
Emperor of the French (1804–1815)

The smeary, thick pressure shows an indulgence of sensuality and, with the falling line, indicates a temperamental, rather depressed individual. The small letters reveal feelings of inferiority but the great underline shows how he compensated for this by behaving in an arrogant, aggressive and attention-seeking manner. He was explosive, single-minded and either silent or overly effusive. Everything about him was intense and distrustful. A man who was determined to make his mark.

Erwin Rommel
German field marshal

With the exception of the pointed top to the capital 'R', we have a series of rounded letters revealing a man who could be aggressive initially in order to get his way but, having achieved that, progressed in a more gentle and co-operative manner. The small loop at the beginning of the 'R' shows him pondering, then the forcefulness of his personality follows. He was undoubtedly a very good leader; see how one stroke gently leads to another, showing how he encouraged and praised others. A logical man and a stubborn one. His final 'l' shows he was in control. The huge top on the 'R' indicates a certain protectiveness.

Joseph Stalin
Soviet leader (1922–1953)

The thick, smeary pressure shows a great intensity of feeling, a vivid imagination and overindulgence of sensuality. The lack of an outlet for this writer's very high energy levels resulted in cruelty, intolerance, brutality and sadism, all confirmed by the club-like strokes at the ends of letters. It is a pedantic type of script, indicating obsessiveness, narrow-mindedness and anger. Explosive outbursts are shown in the

44

ink-filled letters and these would be followed by bouts of silence and depression. A very difficult personality who could not be reasoned with.

Pierre Trudeau
Prime Minister of Canada
(1968–1979; 1980–1984)

A difficult-to-read signature showing a private individual who does not want his innermost thoughts penetrated. It is a speedy, intelligent script and one that shows a calculating mind capable of great tact and diplomacy. It also reveals that he can see into the minds of others but still keep his own thoughts and position hidden. The loop on the 'd' speaks of thoroughness and the large capitals of pride and conceit. A very capable, manipulative individual. This is quite a phallic signature.

Eamon de Valera
President of the Irish Republic (1959–1973)

A very competent, direct and honest person is revealed in the simplicity and clarity of this signature. It shows a good balance between rounded and squared connecting strokes, indicating emotional stability, good powers of observation and an enquiring mentality. The whole shows maturity, imagination and intelligence. The pointed 'm's reveal his penetrating mind and quick grasp of facts. A genuine individual who searched constantly for the truth. The capitals point to good taste and a love of the arts.

POPULAR MUSIC

Adam Ant
Lead singer, Adam and the Ants

Adam Ant

The quite strong pressure here shows a fairly high energy level, and the clear letter formations indicate efficiency and directness. A slight right slant says that the writer enjoys communicating with others but, from the closed 'a', we can see that he is selective in what he has to say. It's a very legible signature, stating 'I am what I am, take it or leave it.' The size is fairly large so he copes well with being in the public eye, but the raised first stroke on the 'n' in 'Ant' reveals that there is something in his day-to-day life that he finds difficult to handle.

John Lennon
Rock musician and songwriter; member of The Beatles

This writer was a moody, restless individual who would invade other people's time and space but was reluctant to give of his own. The erratic baseline shows he could be indecisive, lacking in will power and even, at times, confused between reality and illusion. He had a tendency to be

This is my story both humble an false it to pieces and mend it wil

John Lennon

influenced by others with stronger personalities. He was protective of his family and friends but quite rebellious towards society at large. His greatest gift was his awareness of everything around him, combined with accuracy and precision in his work.

Paul McCartney
Rock musician and songwriter; member of The Beatles

Paul McCartney

A sensitive, caring and creative individual as indicated by the light pressure and thin strokes. He can however be very stubborn – note the straight, long stroke on the capital 'P'. Innovative thinking is shown by the strokes that rise into the upper zone. This is the handwriting of a realistic man who uses all the mental talents available to him. The smallness of the middle-zone letters suggests very good powers of concentration and the desire to tie up all detail himself. The swing of his loops to the left tells us that he relies on his partner for emotional and sexual strength. Certainly the cleverest and most down-to-earth of The Beatles.

George Harrison
Rock guitarist; member of The Beatles

This is very aggressive handwriting indeed, as seen by the repeated angular movements. The 'f' in 'from' tells us the writer has many ideas and gives his all in following them through. The pressure is variable (frequently very heavy), indicating explosive outbursts and mood changes. Basically he has a warm, sensual nature and delights in new experiences. He is very direct and would tell the truth to your face. He is also very physically and materially oriented. A lover of life who is given to hedonism.

Ringo Starr
Drummer; member of The Beatles

This loose, yet connected signature indicates a progressive, unconventional individual who basically does what pleases himself. A certain lack of restraint is seen, together with rebelliousness. Logic, materialism and persistence are all to be found in his powerful 't' crossing. The sharp 'n' shows a man thirsty for information and knowledge. The unusual underline shows confidence, humour and a rude gesture!

Max Bygraves
Entertainer

The gentle right slant shows this writer's desire to communicate his feelings and ideas to others. The 'i' dots are invariably well placed, revealing great attention to detail, and the generally connected script indicates his desire to work in a systematic and well-planned manner. There is little façade to this man; his handwriting and signature are very similar, suggesting little difference between his private and public faces. The 'f's in 'suffice' say he has good ideas and good follow-through – this is known as the letter of practicality. There are a lot of strokes moving in three directions, confirming his great sense of humour, but some movements suggest that he can be unforgiving to those he has disagreed with in the past. A very good friend but a bad enemy.

Dave Clark
Drummer, Dave Clark Five

An aggressive showman with a great sense of humour. This is the writing of a man who is determined to succeed – note the angular 'k' and large capitals – and whose motto is perseverance. The pressure is heavy, indicating a high energy level and the need to make an impression on the world. He is an inspired individual and capable of inspiring others. He varies between script and print, which shows he can be changeable and at times moody, but is always out to achieve. Considerable executive ability is shown.

Jason Donovan
Pop singer and actor

Slanting slightly to the right, this script shows a delightful, pleasant and down-to-earth guy who is as genuine as the image he projects. The pressure indicates a high energy level and the loop at the base of the 's' shows he pushes himself to the limit. This is a balanced script, which tells us that he is a good judge of character, has his feet firmly on the ground and

Yeah, But thats not just
appeal is that energy. Thats
No I think that probably
that applies to everything --
attractive - thats sort of obvi
complements her. But she h
100% concentration - thats at
working with her. But she is
dialogue at home and use
it with each other. And it'd

has the ability to recognise and make the deals that are the most beneficial to him. Satisfaction and the enjoyment of what he does come high on his list of priorities. His lower loops tell us he is not settled on any particular partner but is cautious and will endeavour to pick someone with the long-term view in mind. He loves his food and admires a well-shaped bum!

Sheena Easton
Pop singer

The large, loose, rather erratic script of a lady with a lot of imagination and leadership qualities. She is happiest when involved in large-scale projects and likes being in the driving seat. Restless and very active, she has many ideas, and her firm, high-placed 't' crosses show she has the will power to put these into effect. The very large signature shows her need for recognition, and the inflated lower loops indicate her love of material things. Her sex drive is also strong. Some letters

pull to the left, which suggests she can be cautious and a little sensitive to criticism. The overall impression is of a capable person who loves her work. She also has acting ability. (*Shown slightly reduced.*)

Gary Glitter
Pop singer

This is what is known as mixed-slant writing, indicating constant mood changes. The writer can be friendly and chatty one day whilst avoiding contact and communication the next. (This trait is commonly found in the handwriting of people who were not shown sufficient affection in their formative years.) We can also see a mixture of print and script, which again confirms mood changes and insecurity about his own public image. Quite a few sharp strokes are in evidence, indicating that he can be sarcastic and cynical but is nevertheless thorough in the tasks he undertakes. The 'i'

NAME: *Gary Glitter the 1st*
HEIGHT: *5.8* WEIGHT: *Fluctue* SIGN: *Taurus*
BIRTH DATE: *I Not Tell You* BIRTHPLACE: *BANBURY*
AMBITION: *To get through I think life, with the greatest of ease,*
TURN ONS: *Waking up.*

TURN-OFFS: *Falling asleep on the job.*
FAVOURITE FOOD: *I keep experiencing...*
PREFERRED PERFORMERS: *Exotic taste Read as food.*
ALL TIME FAVE SONG: *Read Performers*
FAVOURITE PASTIME: *Fishing, and pulling people or Person on.*
BEST FILMS: *Ive only made once*
FAVOURITE READING MATTER: *THE WIND & WILL*
FAVOURITE OUTFIT: *EVERY THING NEW*
PERFECT EVENING: *ENTERTAINING on-est with other dinner, or see FAVOURITE*

dots are well placed, showing that he likes to tie up all the details himself. The 't' crosses are quite firm, so he attempts to keep his life on an even keel, although he does not always succeed. He relishes change and variety and has no time for complacency or the mundane. The final swing on the 'r' in 'Glitter' shows he can be a hard taskmaster and sets high standards for both himself and those who work with him. Not an easy partner but always an interesting one.

Elton John
Rock musician and songwriter

A determined and decisive character is exhibited by the lean, straight strokes in this script. A sincere person who is basically serious, shy and, on occasions, irritable. He is a

I am hopeless at drawing

person of regular habits who likes to deal with others in a straightforward, business-minded and ethical manner. He is firm in his resolve and will do what he wants in spite of the consequences. Material gain gives him a great feeling of security and self-worth, yet he is quite spiritual and idealistic. The whole suggests quiet confidence and directness.

Simon Le Bon
Lead singer, Duran Duran

Hello, just thought I'd write. to say that we're still alive, a an Idea of what we'll be doin coming year. After a world tour. been virtually non stop since Ma in our ...

An intelligent, clear-thinking individual who communicates best with people well known to him, as seen by the slight right slant combined with closed 'a's and 'o's. All his 'I's look like musical notes, which confirms his talent for, and love of, music. His loops are full, showing his capacity for a loving sexual relationship, and the baseline is straight and even,

54

indicating a sense of responsibility. The accuracy with which he places his 'i' dots reveals his attentiveness to detail. A well-balanced personality.

Kylie Minogue
Pop singer and actress

A lovely, cheerful individual who enjoys whatever she is doing at the time, as shown by the uprightness of her handwriting. Today is what matters to her. One of her talents, seen by her rounded baseline, is to remain charming even if she feels she is surrounded by idiots. The large middle-zone letters tell us her assurance borders on presumptuousness and conceit, and she tends to exaggerate trivia. She is self-protective and always has a quick, ready answer, revealed by the reversed 'd'. The looped and knotted 't's show perseverance and tenacity. The whole speaks of a love of movement and activity, and the heavy pressure confirms she has the energy to go with it. The 'y' loops are swinging to the left, showing her sexual restlessness and the need for change and variety.

Elvis Presley
Rock-and-roll singer and originator

The connection of the Christian name with the surname shows this writer's desire to project his own image. He was quite a positive person and was in an optimistic frame of mind at the time of writing this sample. This is shown by the rising 'ley' in 'Presley'. It is a warm, friendly and proud signature. Humour is revealed in the three-way movement of the 'P'. He was emotional, artistic and had a high, restless energy level. His sex drive was strong but because of the pull of the 'y' to the left we know that he relied on a partner for encouragement to express his sexuality.

Cliff Richard
Pop singer

The pressure of this writing shows a lot of warmth and humour. Very simple, clear-cut strokes state that the writer is direct and honest in his dealings with others. The accurately placed 'i' dots and 't' crosses tell us he has an eye for detail, and the disconnected nature of much of the script reveals someone with a lot of intuition, who invariably knows what is right for himself. The cruciform shape of the 't's confirms his religious convictions and the pull of the 'y' to the left suggests that he sublimates his sexual drive in helping other people. A nice, genuine individual.

Roger Whittaker
Popular singer

The large, inflated 'R' of the showman but the small letters of a businessman. This is the handwriting of a quick-thinking, clever man, who outwardly shows a great deal of self-assurance. Because of the smallness of the middle-zone letters, we see someone who likes to keep his finger on the pulse of everything he is involved in. Delegating does not come easily to him and he likes to tie up all the details himself. He has a need for privacy in his personal life and guards his family and friends well. He comes alive on stage but experiences little difficulty in reverting to the role of family

To Gloria

with every good wish

Roger Whittaker

man and father. He requires peace and quiet at home in order
to function at his best when in the public eye.

Toyah Willcox
Rock singer and actress

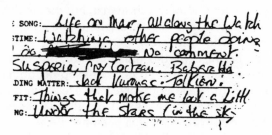

The Greek 'e' shows this writer's love of culture and, combined with the disconnections in her words, reveals literary
ability. This is sharp handwriting indicating a critical nature.
She sets high standards both for herself and those around
her, and is frequently disappointed in her fellow humans,
who are not as thorough as she is. She tends to jump into
situations where a little more preliminary thought would be
a good idea. Her 't' crosses show she can be self-indulgent
and, on occasions, get her priorities wrong. She enjoys
reading, as seen by the printed 's', when she gets the time,
but she experiences some difficulty in relaxing. A clever,
intelligent girl who would benefit from letting go of the past.
She has many good ideas but insufficient follow-through.

SPORT

George Best
Footballer (Northern Ireland)

The gigantic size of this signature tells of excessive pride; here is someone who must be seen and heard. His tastes lean to the grandiose, luxurious and flamboyant, and he is extravagant, wayward and restless. He is most suited to working in television or the theatre – somewhere he can attract a large audience. Some lack of reality is in evidence. He is a very stubborn man who always feels he knows what is best. His lovely sense of humour is clearly evident, as is his warm and ardent nature. He has a superior attitude but is nonetheless a great showman.

Shirley Crabtree ('Big Daddy')
Wrestler

The showman of all showmen! Not one hint of aggression in the whole script. This is a man who thrives on recognition, acclaim and the applause of the audience. The tall upper loops tell of his high intelligence and the preliminary strokes in 'Best', 'Big' and 'Daddy' scream, 'Put me on a platform!' He is quite emotional and would feel genuinely upset if he hurt anyone. A lovely guy with great curiosity, he has good business sense and likes being involved in large-scale projects. (*Shown slightly reduced*.)

Jimmy Greaves
Footballer (England) and television presenter

[handwritten signature text]

A very intuitive individual who is better at solving other people's problems than his own. He loves giving advice but is not much good at accepting it! This is predominantly an upright script, which tells us he is self-reliant and has leadership qualities. However, as some of the lower loops pull to the left we can see that he relies on his partner for emotional strength. A close family relationship is very important to him. The many straight strokes indicate efficiency and the desire to be clearly understood. He has a pleasant manner and neither over- nor underestimates his own abilities. His 't' crosses remind one of head-butting but actually reveal a desire to be in control.

Bruce Grobbelaar
Goalkeeper (Liverpool FC)

This medium-sized handwriting tells us that the writer's imagination is never divorced from reality. He concentrates well and prefers to be practical and constructive. He lives very much for today and is quite a charmer, too. There is a lot of roundness in the writing, which indicates that he has his lazy days and also that he dislikes arguments or friction.

> *when MR Rea came out of his way to collect them. He was to take everything back to the Cayman Islands the next day to raise money for charity.*

However, because of the narrowness of some of the letters we see that he can become uptight and anxious under pressure. A Mr Nice-Guy who is proud of his achievements to date.

Gary Player
Golfer

> *hope to have in one day.*
>
> *Sincerely,*
>
> *Gary Player.*

The right slant reveals this person's friendly and sociable nature. An emotionally healthy individual who is even-tempered, well-organised and clear-thinking. He has a keen mind and considerable executive ability. There is very good balance to the writing, showing he likes to give equal attention to all areas of his life. The additional starting strokes indicate caution and preliminary thinking before undertaking any task. The 'P' in 'Player' is whip-like and shows that he drives himself hard and always plays to win! He behaves exactly the same in private as in public.

Tessa Sanderson
Javelin thrower and heptathlete

The left slant here reveals a cautious lady who thinks before she acts. Her reversed 'd' in 'today' tells us that she is self-protective and dislikes being questioned about her moods or motives. The very angular lower loops show her high energy level, sporting interests and strong sex drive. The whole, however, suggests a lot of frustration in that she desires to be more progressive but is held back by negative past experiences which she cannot let go of. She is unsure of her self-image and finds criticism hard to take. She is both angry and confused but also very loyal and kind to her close friends.

Barry Sheen
Racing motorcyclist

This large handwriting speaks of a flamboyant person, who welcomes recognition. Part of the 'w' is eliminated,

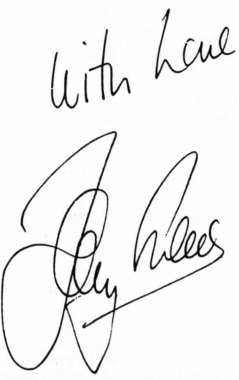

indicating that there is something in his day-to-day life that he finds unacceptable. The hook on the 'l' in 'love' hints at hoarding instincts. He is intelligent and has original ideas. The complicated and illegible signature reveals pride and also a lack of trust. He can be very suspicious of the moods and motives of others. The underline shows confidence and the full stop says 'Listen to me!'

Mark Spitz
Swimmer

There are some very unusual formations here, showing a great deal of originality in thought and action. Strong 't' crosses indicate the writer's will power and ability to get things done. The pressure shows warmth and humour, but the endstroke on the 'z' reveals some disappointment in personal relationships. From the extension on the 'k' we can see his generosity, while the initial stroke instead of an 'M' is a sign of inquisitiveness and a thirst for knowledge.

STAGE AND SCREEN

Jane Asher
Actress and author (*Wish Me Luck*, etc.)

[handwritten note]
> Just a note
> you would still
> drawing of me by
> are we too late.
> She's very kee

The handwriting of a reserved and spiritual individual. Great delicacy of feeling is revealed here. Her dislike of arguments or conflict is shown by the clean, light strokes. A refined person and a lover of all the arts. Very good word and line spacing showing planning and organising ability. This well-balanced script indicates good judgement and intuition. An articulate individual who speaks quietly, sincerely and positively, she sees essentials, acts upon them and makes little fuss or noise. Vulgarity has no appeal whatsoever. A culture vulture!

Warren Beatty
Film actor (*Bonnie and Clyde*; *Reds*)

A gentle, charming individual, as revealed by the roundness

of the script. He is, however, quite persistent and progressive – note the right slant. The handwriting is mostly connected, showing his logical approach and his ability to work in a systematic manner, while the fullness indicates a colourful imagination and a flexibility in his attitude to others. Here is someone who is animated and vivacious. He has a relaxed nature and does not take life too seriously. Possessing a good visual memory, he is able to give a vivid description of an experience. On a more negative note, he may sometimes indulge in fantasies. A loving character with a great sense of humour. (*Shown slightly reduced.*)

Ingrid Bergman
Film actress (*For Whom the Bell Tolls; Casablanca*)

A person of high ideals, whose fellow humans seldom matched up to the high standards she set for them. The pressure is quite light, indicating a sensitive nature and a certain delicacy of feeling. She disliked rudeness or coarseness and was very much a lady. At times she allowed herself to be dominated by others with stronger personalities. She was tolerant, genial and spiritual. The narrowness of some of the letters speaks of a practical nature and a liking for order and tidiness. However, it also indicates her inhibitions

[handwritten note]

in personal relationships. She was ambitious but procrastination, as shown by the 't' crosses that fail to cross the stems, did not permit her to achieve all her aims and desires.

Michael Caine
Film actor (*The Ipcress File; Educating Rita*)

Very connected writing, showing this person's logical, rational approach to everything. He has an enquiring mind but sometimes experiences difficulty in communicating just how intelligent he is. He has very good powers of concentration and a good memory for facts, although regarding day-to-day obligations he can be quite forgetful. This is the sharp handwriting of someone intense and rather rigid in his beliefs. The letters decrease in size at the ends of words, showing that he is manipulative and has a tendency to want things done his way. The 'i' dots pull very much to the right – a sign of impatience. A loyal man and protective of those close to him, he admires efficiency and does not suffer fools gladly. He is selective in his friendships.

Charlie (Sir Charles) Chaplin
Comedian, film actor and director
(*The Gold Rush; The Great Dictator*)

A surprisingly moody and oversensitive person who was very critical of both himself and others (seen by the sharpness of the strokes). The angles on the 't's indicate obstinacy and the desire to have his own way. His judgement of other people was good but he formed strong likes or dislikes based on first impressions. He kept his emotions very much under control and experienced difficulty in communicating intimately with anyone. Basically he was an austere, cleanliness-conscious individual who was never satisfied with his performance. However, he was very protective towards those he loved.

Joan Collins
Film and television actress (*The Bitch*; *Dynasty*)

A tremendously warm and sensual nature is shown here. The writer delights in all of her five senses, as seen by the pressure of the script. Her 'a's and 'o's are closed, showing discretion, and the full loops reveal her emotional nature. Her tying together of 'Joan' and 'Collins' tells us she likes to make the maximum use of her personality and will use her charm and wiliness to gain control. This is not a woman to argue with; she is very persistent, and she always plans for the future. She is frank, honest, direct and has a big ego. Her business acumen is considerable. She has a genuinely warm and friendly nature, welcomes a challenge and is very forward-thinking. Beauty delights her in all its shapes and forms.

Sean Connery
Film actor (James Bond in various films; *The Untouchables*)

This is the handwriting of a very charming individual, as shown by the roundness of the script. The pressure tells of a

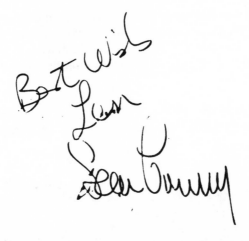

relaxed personality – someone who behaves the same in private as in public. He welcomes hard work, as indicated by the additional loops at the bases of 'Best' and 'Sean'. The slant wavers sometimes, so he can be moody but he quickly recovers. The uprightness tells us that his emotions are very much under control and that he is independent and self-reliant. One of his most attractive qualities is his dry wit. A delightful, loyal individual.

Sir Noël Coward
Dramatist, actor, composer and film director

This writer's strokes go in three directions, indicating a great sense of humour and a talent for mimicry. A very flamboyant signature, revealing his love of recognition and need to be noticed. Some pulls to the left show that he was nostalgic and liked to talk about the 'good old days'. He was a stubborn person and was not easily swayed. The beginning of the 'N' is a distinct phallic symbol. He could be very charming, but at other times irritable and standoffish. He delighted in gaiety and frivolity, but his reactions were frequently unpredictable.

Joan Crawford
Film actress (*Mildred Pierce; Whatever Happened to Baby Jane?*)

A lady with an alert, speedy mind, indicated by the slant to the right and the quick script. The very strong 't' crosses tell of her tenacity, persistence and desire to overcome all obstacles placed in her way. This was someone who never avoided a challenge; in fact it drove her to greater effort. She was restless, impatient and greedy, loved material possessions (note the very full lower zone) and constantly sought recognition. She was flamboyant, extroverted and attention-seeking. She could be uptight (some narrow letters) and moody, and often got her priorities wrong. The loops running into each other tell us she was accident prone but extremely energetic. An active and fulfilling sex life was important to her. The pointed underline speaks of a strong dislike of interference in her personal life. (*Shown slightly reduced.*)

Bette Davis
Film actress (*Jezebel; Whatever Happened to Baby Jane?*)

[handwritten text] prompted you to write — & may lips very performace may continue to please!

Sincerely

Bette Davis

The rising lines show great enthusiasm for life. The rounded bases of the letters combined with the pointed tops (particularly on the 'm's) give a good clue that here was someone intellectually, but not emotionally, mature. Charm is in evidence, but behind an iron fist! The spiky 'p's suggest a very argumentative nature. She was a perfectionist who always liked to get her own way. Her 't' crosses fly to the right, showing intolerance of those less quick-thinking than herself. She had a love of the arts and of beauty, as seen by her Greek 'e's. Great impatience is shown; she wanted everything done yesterday.

Edward Fox
Film and television actor (*The Day of the Jackal; Edward and Mrs Simpson*)

Here we have a very clever combination of both angular and thread-like movements, showing that the writer is receptive to new ideas and thorough in everything he does. He is a perfectionist with a tendency to simplify issues. The starting stroke on the 'm' reveals scepticism, and the extremely small 'i' tells us he feels he has not achieved his full potential. He is

With my best wishes.

Yours Sincerely . Edward Fox

articulate but cautious with words. An idealistic man who can appear very remote. The whole suggests he is dissatisfied with his success to date. Total accuracy is vital to him.

Liza Goddard
Stage and television actress (*Bergerac*, etc.)

Very light pressure and very large handwriting – this is in fact the perfect writing for the actor/actress who enjoys taking

Best wishes

Liza Goddard x

on the role of another. It also indicates sensitivity and delicacy of feeling. These types are completely lacking in inhibition, but can sometimes allow others with a stronger personality to dominate them. They tend not to learn from past experiences but are invariably pleasant, charming and a joy to have around. This person welcomes and enjoys all the recognition she receives.

Nigel Hawthorne
Stage and television actor (*Yes, Minister;
The Barchester Chronicles*)

[handwritten text]

This is someone who works efficiently and with great precision, despite the fact that he is not naturally gifted with a lot of energy. It is a very right-slanting script which shows he enjoys giving vent to his feelings. Its connectedness tells of his good memory for factual detail. This is very intelligent, simplified handwriting, showing a direct and natural manner. His taste is quite austere and he likes to be surrounded by well-chosen objects. Vulgarity and loud colours are abhorrent to him. A lot of reserve is seen and the wide word spacing tells of the writer's need for privacy. He is very discriminating in his choice of friends.

Bernard Hepton
Television actor (*The Secret Army;
Tinker, Tailor, Soldier, Spy*)

*started well but
: appearing and there
in Eater. Let's hope*

Bernard Hepton

The pressure in this script tells of the writer's warmth and sense of humour. The slant varies slightly, which indicates that he can be moody: communicative one day, less so the next. The 'n's are broad, revealing his expansiveness in social situations. He enjoys travel and is kindly to the underdog. He does not like to be questioned about his movements and can be stubborn. The last letters of his words tend to be disconnected, suggesting that he often starts things he does not finish. Very little movement in the lower zone, showing a lack of interest in material things; not too much energy for sex but he may like a tipple!

Dustin Hoffman
Film actor (*The Graduate; Tootsie*)

A very determined individual who will leave no stone unturned in the pursuit of his own interests. A lot of mental energy and aggression is shown, as is an extremely positive attitude to life. His pen does not leave the paper, which indicates an angry obstinacy and persistence. His 't' cross shows imagination and the endstroke suggests he will keep at bay anyone who tries to hinder him. He is motivated by material gain and also has a strong sex drive. Both sceptical and critical, he will not hesitate to speak his mind. An achiever.

Princess Grace of Monaco
Film actress (as Grace Kelly)

Not a very inspiring signature for such a gracious lady. Its roundness shows her charm and the openings on the 'o's suggest oratory ability, but it is all rather copybook in style, indicating a preference for conventional and generally accepted standards of behaviour. Socially she was friendly but aloof. She was unadventurous but conscientious and co-operative, and had a very healthy respect for rules and regulations. Only in the 'G' of 'Grace' do we see any signs of self-assertion, but even these are quite mild. A lady who would have found difficulty in adapting to the changing face of modern society.

Sophia Loren
Film actress (*The Millionairess;
The Cassandra Crossing*)

Mental agility is revealed here by the directness of the

strokes. The loops are full, showing the writer can be very emotional, and the majority of the 'o's are knotted, suggesting a secretive nature. However, this is a lady who comes straight to the point and says exactly what she has to say. She does not suffer fools gladly and because of the size of her handwriting we know she enjoys acclaim and recognition. The signature is somewhat illegible, confirming her desire to keep her innermost thoughts to herself. An individual who is difficult to get to know but always charming on a superficial level.

Joanna Lumley
Actress and television personality (*The New Avengers*, etc.)

The very strong, thick pressure here shows a lady of warmth and humour. The connectedness of her signature indicates that she is logical, while the knot on the 'e' tells us she can be guarded and secretive. From the size of the writing we can see that she needs recognition, is very ambitious and dislikes spending long periods of time alone. The pointed tops on the 'm' show an enquiring mentality; this is someone who likes to have answers even to the inexplicable. The large, swinging loop on the 'y' shows a high energy level and sexual adventurousness.

Virginia McKenna
Film actress and animal-rights campaigner
(*Carve Her Name with Pride; Born Free*)

A charming, delightful lady with great delicacy of feeling. This is a sensitive person who has no time in her life for anger, friction or aggressiveness. She has definite ideas and will work hard to achieve her aims, but in a direct, honest and matter-of-fact way. She is never two-faced and behaves the same with everyone. The simplicity of her strokes shows efficiency and a love of culture. The little crossing on the 'y' tells us she is very romantic and is in love with the idea of being in love.

Marilyn Monroe
Film actress (*Lets Make Love; Some Like It Hot*)

This right-slanting script shows someone who loved communicating with others and was quite modern in her thinking. She was enthusiastic, restless and filled with nervous energy. She loved activity and was driven by strong sexual urges which could at times dominate her life. These are shown by the long lower loops running into the words below. When these urges overtook her, she was like a child and wanted instant gratification. The long endstroke on 'seeing' suggests that she felt threatened. She was a very

80

*You will be
seeing more of me
soon in -
"Let's Make Love"*

Marilyn

warm, affectionate lady but all the ink-filled ovals tell of
explosive outbursts and a tendency to excess, not just in
matters of sex, but in food and drink too. The very involved
'M' in 'Marilyn' indicates absorption with self and great
vanity. The lack of pressure on the right-hand side of the 'l'
reveals her great insecurity about the future.

Pat Phoenix
Television actress (Elsie Tanner in *Coronation
Street*)

A rhythmic type of signature, showing someone who tried to
find smooth solutions to difficult problems. Some angular
movements in the small letters indicate that underneath a soft

front was quite a tough lady. The rounded tops to the capitals show a protectiveness towards those close to her and the ability to project her own personality and use it to the maximum effect. Some compulsiveness is seen, as is determination and intelligence. A mixture here of strength and vulnerability.

Vincent Price
Film actor (*House of Wax; The Fall of the House of Usher*)

A very interesting script; the narrow letters and the wide spacing between them clearly indicate that although this writer is outwardly an extrovert character, underneath he is uptight, somewhat introverted and very cautious when expressing his feelings. The tick stroke at the beginning of 'suddenly' shows him clinging to old ideas, finding difficulty in looking to the future. Humour of a dry nature is shown, and he likes to take the lead and to stand out in a crowd, but he is not too comfortable with himself. The whip-like movements indicate a slightly cruel and controlling nature, but also an artistic one.

Dave Prowse
Film and television actor (Darth Vader in *Star Wars*)

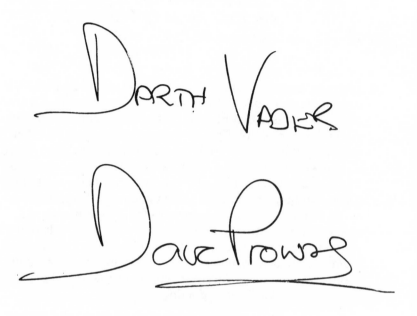

The very large writing of someone who is a great attention seeker, loves working in the public eye and is at his best when being observed. It is quite an angular script, revealing a lot of determination and mental aggression. The long starting strokes leading in to 'Darth' and 'Dave' show someone who thrives on a platform and needs an audience to come alive. The large capitals also indicate a lot of self-confidence and feelings of pride in his achievements. The reverse underline is a sign that he likes to keep his family and children away from the public eye. A capable man, who will give his all in order to succeed in whatever career he takes on. Many leadership qualities are shown. (*Shown slightly reduced.*)

Oliver Reed
Film actor (*Women in Love; Castaway*)

The rightward slant shows this writer's love of communication, but as the majority of his 'a's and 'o's are closed we can see that he will communicate with others only when he wants to. The 'd's always swing to the left, indicating that he is very self-protective and will always have a quick, ready reply and a good excuse for his misdemeanours. There is a lot of humour and bravado to the script, but because of the very high and firm 't' crossings we find a man who is protective towards family and friends alike. He produces a strong, unusually shaped 'p' in 'pleased', showing he can be sexually athletic. His letters vary in size, giving a good clue to mood changes and variations in his own feelings of self-worth. An attractive, larger-than-life character who would be difficult to pin down.

Burt Reynolds
Film actor (*Deliverance; Smokey and the Bandit*)

The large capital letters here show pride, ambition and the desire for recognition. The full loops tell us he is an emotional man who becomes deeply involved in any part he plays. He is very logical, as shown by the connectedness of the script, and will become irritated if interrupted during the course of his work. It is also an aesthetic script, indicating his love of beauty and beautiful surroundings. This is a romantic man with a great sense of humour. The long, extended endstrokes show his discrimination when forming close relationships. He values greatly those whom he trusts.

Frank Sinatra
Singer and film actor (*From Here to Eternity;*
High Society)

A flowing signature which reveals the writer's easy co-ordination. An intelligent man who can be both manipulative and diplomatic. He faces problems head-on and is a good, speedy decision maker. He dislikes procrastination and can be very impatient. The 'S', rather like an egg timer, tells us that he has a strong dislike of the ageing process! The reversed loop on the 'k' in 'Frank' speaks of his rebelliousness and occasional desire to shock.

Terence Stamp
Film actor (*Billy Budd; Far from the Madding*
Crowd)

The very thread-like writing gives a great clue to this man's

restless and curious nature. He has a hunger for new experiences but finds difficulty in communicating his thoughts and feelings to others. He is a gentle and wandering spirit and, like his signature, is either riding on the crest of a wave or quietly pondering. He will seek the companionship of original and imaginative people and will not allow himself to give way to anger or aggression. He views the world from a wide perspective.

Elizabeth Taylor
Film actress (*Cat on a Hot Tin Roof*; *Who's Afraid of Virginia Woolf?*)

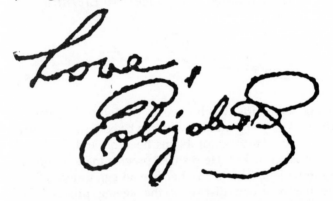

This rising signature clearly shows the writer's professional ambition. The swinging 'L' in 'Love' reveals her charisma, charm and sense of humour, while the inflated 'E' in 'Elizabeth' indicates a need to attract attention and a love of public adoration. The 'z' shows a strong sex drive and the extension on the 'e' in 'Love' says that she is generous and likes to give to those she loves. She can be quite vulgar and enjoys storytelling, often embroidered for good effect. The pressure of the writing tells of her warmth, but it is also erratic, showing varying energy levels. A lot of emotion is seen here, but she is also a great flirt.

John Wayne
Film actor (*Stagecoach; True Grit*)

This was a very domineering and aggressive man, as shown by the angular movements in the writing. He made a great impression on his surroundings and demanded notice and attention at all times. He had an abundance of energy, a strong will and, despite his outward appearance, frequently felt uptight, cautious and ill-at-ease. Sarcasm and a cynical attitude are in evidence, as is the ability to subdue others with a few well-chosen words. His sex drive was strong but so was his sense of dissatisfaction and frustration.

Barbara Windsor
Film actress (*Carry on Cabby*, etc.)

There are very small spaces between the words in this script, indicating that here is someone who will crowd others for attention. She needs closeness and affection but can experience some difficulty in returning such warmth. She knots a lot of her letters, telling of her inflexibility, while the 'g' in 'Plough' suggests a great deal of sexual vanity. She actually enjoys displaying her physical attributes and her motto is, 'If you've got it, flaunt it!' A Peter-Pan lady with a great sense of humour. She is a good mimic too.

THE ROYAL FAMILY

Her Majesty Queen Elizabeth II

The Queen's regal signature shows us that she is comfortable with her position. She is very clear-thinking – note the simplification of the letter formations – and her firm 't' cross shows a strong will. The unadorned capital 'E' indicates her refinement, gentleness and love of cultural pursuits. It is slightly narrow handwriting, suggesting that she experiences some difficulty in relaxing. The loops show thoroughness and controlled emotion. She is idealistic and demands a lot of herself.

Her Majesty Queen Elizabeth the Queen Mother

This large, imposing signature is much as one would expect from royalty, and shows the Queen Mother's regal and leadership qualities. Its clarity speaks of directness and the steady baseline reveals her reliability and emotional stability. The leftward pull on the capital 'E' indicates self-confidence, self-reliance and independence, and also shows her motherly instincts. The whole indicates her love of, and comfort with, pomp and ceremony. This signature is very similar to that of the Queen, and we can see that both writers are happy in their roles.

HRH The Duke of Edinburgh

Prince Philip's signature is written with very firm, straight strokes, showing his direct, no-nonsense attitude. 'If you have something to say, say it,' is his motto. He has a strong dislike of waffle and time wasting and does not suffer fools gladly. He can be both impatient and critical, and is very logical, so appeals to him must be based on facts not emotion. He has high ideals and sets high standards for himself and others, as shown by the tall upper-zone letters. He is very curious – note the high 'i' dots – and has good powers of observation. Great loyalty is shown and also a high energy level. The leanness of the writing tells us that he is seldom interested in anything that does not serve a useful purpose.

HRH The Prince of Wales

This writing, which slants to the left, shows caution and extreme sensitivity. Prince Charles takes offence easily and his emotions are not to be tampered with. There is a strong

Charles (signature)

mother influence and we can see that he experiences great difficulty in accepting change or progress. He can be charming in social situations but finds it hard to express emotion. His tightly knotted 'o's reveal that he is sometimes secretive and crafty. He likes his own way, shows a lot of independence and invariably keeps those close to him at arm's length. He has a fair degree of energy and always pushes himself to the limit. As a lover he can be self-centred and somewhat unadventurous.

HRH The Princess of Wales

With endless gratitude & thanks — Diana (handwritten inscription)

This is the handwriting of one who lives very much for today; whatever activity she is involved in at a given moment is undertaken gracefully and with interest. She is very charming, as illustrated by the roundness of the script. The rather large 'a's say that she can be quite possessive in her relationships with friends and partner alike. It is important to her to be needed and she cares what others think of her. She is quick-thinking but not particularly original. The broadness of the writing shows a need for freedom in thought and action. It is very important to her to communicate openly with others. Undoubtedly the greatest difficulty she will experience in her marriage to Prince Charles is his lack of readiness to relate closely and intimately with her. Outward displays of affection are also necessary to her.

HRH The Princess Royal

Dear Ann,

Thank you so much for your invitation — I'd love to come on Dec. 18th, perhaps nearer the date

Yours sincerely,

Anne

The handwriting of a no-nonsense lady. She speaks her mind but surprisingly is more sensitive to criticism than she would ever let the world know (shown by the looped 'd's). She will actually stew about slights or insults but will never admit this to anyone. She has a tough exterior but a soft core! Very firm strokes tell us she is a dedicated, thorough achiever who gives her all to anything she undertakes. The very tall capitals show how she sets out with a high degree of confidence but invariably feels dissatisfied with the end result. The uprightness of the script shows a loyal individual who values family and close friends greatly. A good, strong sex drive is indicated by the deep, long strokes in the lower zone.

Captain Mark Phillips

This fairly small signature with compensating large capitals reveals a reasonably outgoing person who is outwardly confident but basically rather reserved and happiest when working by himself. His tall letters are a sign of idealism, and the gaps between the letters show a great deal of intuition and perception. His ideas are very personal. He can be critical of others but has little insight into his own feelings. He may at times be rather anti-social. The narrow 'p' in 'Phillips' shows repressed sexuality, but the rising signature and small underline reveal cautious optimism.

HRH The Duke of York

The rather old-fashioned capital 'A' shows Prince Andrew's respect for tradition, and the rounded baseline his ability to remain charming in social situations. Three-way movements indicate a sense of humour, but the reversed small 'r' tells us that he can sometimes be touchy or oversensitive. He is independent by nature and will make his own decisions. A very loyal and steadfast individual who is protective towards his family and friends. The broadness of the 'w' indicates ambition and courage, while the pressure shows a warm and loving person who likes surprising his partner.

HRH The Duchess of York

Like her signature, the Duchess is bouncy and plunges enthusiastically into anything she undertakes. She is

Sarah Ferguson.

observant, as shown by the gap after the capital 'S'. More intuitive than other members of the royal family, she follows her instincts and can size up people and situations very quickly. Her basic desire is to offer the hand of friendship to those who wish to take it. A very pleasant individual, not always the most tactful but sincere and honest. She is warm and loving, has a great sense of humour and does not take life too seriously. A good partner and ideally suited to her husband.

HRH The Prince Edward

Edward

Quite a broad signature, indicating someone who needs space in which to spread himself and feels confined in small areas. Prince Edward can be a little shy but is nonetheless drawn towards people. The variable pressure suggests mood swings, and the small 'x' in the capital 'E' gives us a clue to his critical nature. He is quite charming but has a tendency to depression. He does not seek the limelight and is more comfortable with people he knows well. He communicates fluently but in a quiet manner.

HRH The Princess Margaret

The second descending stroke on the 'M' tells us of Princess Margaret's stubborn nature and her desire to get her own way. The middle-zone letters show how charming she can be, but they also indicate secretiveness. She dislikes being questioned closely and the looped 't' suggests that she can be sensitive and take offence easily. The removed 't' cross reveals impatience and, at times, a very condescending attitude. The firm, strong underline says, 'I am a princess, do not forget it.'

HRH Princess Alexandra

A very direct, straightforward attitude is shown in this signature. The large letters tell us that Princess Alexandra enjoys her prominent position in public life, but the 'x' suggests she can, at times, feel weighed down by responsibility. There is humour in the 'd' movement and also a love of music. The simplicity of the 'A' shows efficiency and cultural awareness, while the combination of connected and disconnected letters reveals a good balance between logical and intuitive thinking, which enables her to fulfil many of her desires and ambitions.

Your Personality Revealed

Self-Analysis Through Handwriting

For Peggy, whose help is invaluable; Janet, Anne, Gillian, Pamela, Jenny and Marabelle, who have assisted me on my lecture tours around the world

CONTENTS

INTRODUCTION

How do you function in your chosen career? Are you a good decision maker? Do you have leadership qualities? What is your attention to detail like? In personal relationships, do you consider your partner's feelings? Perhaps you are the happy-go-lucky type, but does this pay the bills? Do you consider your children a joy and pleasure, or are they getting in the way of your doing just what you want to do? Are you creative, do you enjoy sport, or are you the greatest of lovers?

Have you been making accurate assessments of yourself and others? You may have been amazed when others have let you down when you have always considered yourself such a good judge of character. Perhaps, at times, your own actions or reactions amaze you.

It is time to rediscover who you really are and what motivates you. The human personality is extremely complex and one of the greatest aids to understanding oneself and others is handwriting analysis. Now you can analyse your own handwriting.

Graphology, or handwriting analysis, is the study of handwriting movements for the purpose of determining the personality of the writer. No two people write exactly the same – even twins write differently.

Handwriting is actually brainwriting; we merely use our hands as a tool to produce our particular script. There has been for many years now an established body of knowledge on which handwriting analysis is based and the same rules are applied worldwide.

Age cannot be determined with total accuracy. A person's actual age is often at variance with his mental age – you meet mature 14-year-olds and immature 50-year-olds! The sex of a person is another difficult area to determine, as we all have masculine as well as feminine traits in our makeup.

7

Left-handedness makes little difference, since as many lefthanders as righthanders produce a right slanting script. Perhaps you have noticed how they adjust the paper, or their position, in order to do this. People who have lost the use of one hand and are forced to use the other generally develop a writing style that closely resembles their earlier one, unless of course their personality has changed. Graphology is not predictive but it can clearly show your potential.

Fast handwriting suggests a greater degree of naturalness, genuineness and spontaneity; while slow writing, in an adult, reveals a more self-conscious, calculating personality.

This book is divided into two sections. Section I sets out the interpretations of the dominant movements. These are the movements that immediately strike you as you look at a sample. Section II gives interpretations of the secondary, or lesser movements. These will be evident on closer inspection of the writing. A movement that appears occasionally shows a tendency; if it appears often it shows a habit. And, if it appears constantly, it is an integral part of the personality. The human personality is full of contradictions and you may find that some of the interpretations are too. But this is simply an indication that no one is totally extrovert or totally introvert; completely selfish or unselfish, but that we are all made up of a mixture of positive and negative traits. As a result, no one should ever be afraid of having their handwriting analysed – we are each as good as the next person, just different.

All you need to do to get the maximum benefit from this book is to:

1) produce a sample of handwriting on unlined paper (approximately 50 words is ideal);
2) choose the dominant movements from Section I that immediately strike you on looking at the sample;
3) choose the secondary movements from Section II

that you find on closer inspection;
4) combine the two for the analysis that is uniquely yours.

It is preferable to use a sample not specifically written for this exercise and produced with the pen the writer is most comfortable with.

THE FOLLOWING ARE EXAMPLES OF SCRIPTS WITH THEIR DOMINANT AND SECONDARY MOVEMENTS INDICATED.

1. **Large size.** *Dominant lower zone. Right slant. Triangular g and y. Long t crosses.*

2. **Totally disconnected.** *Pasty pressure. Accurate i dots. o's open to right.*

3. **Angular letter shapes.** *Connected. Single stroke personal pronoun 'I'. Accurate i dots.*

9

all quite silly but I
spelling to have to do
I writ the way I read

4. **Varying sized letters.** *Uneven baseline. Very small personal pronoun 'I'. Loops on t's.*

To tell you a little
my own personality -
am an introvent or a

5. **Arcade letter shapes.** *Dominant middle zone. Words too close together. i dots to right.*

The quick brown fox
Jumped over the lazy
dog.

6. **Balanced zones.** Garland letter shapes. Simplified writing style. Good word and line spacing.

SECTION I

Dominant Movements

11

1

Size

Size	3 mm 3 mm 3 mm
large	9½ mm plus
medium	9 mm
small	8½ mm or less
Varying size	

LARGE

I am having a drink
bar; now I have h

If you have large handwriting, you are extroverted, extravagant and must excel in whatever you do. The intensity of your drive is greater the larger your script. You have strong feelings of self-importance and are prone to bouts of exhibitionism. You are very imaginative, need variety and plenty of activity. You also have a yearning

12

for power and the desire to dominate others. Your leadership qualities are considerable and material possessions mean a great deal to you. On the negative side, you can be too bossy, inattentive to detail, and absent-minded. Your extravagance can get you into financial difficulty and your constant need for a new challenge makes you restless, careless and often tactless.

In business You are only comfortable in the boss's seat, have fine leadership qualities and are never short of new ideas. You will command respect and can be intolerant of others who do not match up to the standards you set for them.

As a lover You are great: imaginative, and fond of variety. You do everything on a grand scale and are likely to whisk a lover off to Paris or Rome for a quick lunch! You love buying expensive gifts, and you expect the same in return. When life becomes dull or boring with a particular partner who is not adventurous, you do have the tendency to move on!

As a parent You want the very best for your children and will encourage and praise them when they do well. Money will always be made available for extra activities, such as horse riding, skiing, school outings and dance classes. It is always a two-way deal with you: you do your best; we'll give you the means to do it!

MEDIUM

What a lovely party!
did so enjoy it all.
you must have worked

If you have a medium-sized script, you tend to be conventional and fit in with prevailing circumstances. You

13

neither over- nor underestimate your own abilities. Too much responsibility is unwelcome and you are most comfortable in a position as second-in-command, or as an assistant. You find a certain amount of routine appealing and your mind is rarely divorced from reality. You are usually practical and realistic, with your feet firmly on the ground, but sometimes you limit yourself and could explore life more fully.

In business A doer rather than a thinker, you would make an excellent personal assistant – no one need worry that you are after their job! You are frequently delightful and pleasant to all around you, unless pushed to do what you consider is beyond your capabilities or sphere of responsibility. You need a degree of comfort and steadiness in everything you do.

As a lover Security comes high on your list of priorities. You like the 'tried and trusted' and tend to stay with one partner as long as life is reasonably comfortable. Friday-night sex after the pub on a weekly basis could well be acceptable to you. You are not necessarily boring but like planning and organization in your life. Extravagant gestures have little appeal but genuine acts of kindness are greatly appreciated. You show great respect to a good provider.

As a parent On the whole, you are a good parent, since your kind disposition makes you conscious of your children's needs. You encourage a child to do his/her best and set no hard or fast rules. You will show extreme pride if one of your offspring does particularly well in anything. On the whole, yours is a comfortable family situation.

Mary had a little lambs
Its fleece was white as snow
And everywhere that Mary went
The lambs was sure to go

Small writing is that of shy and modest people who rarely seek the limelight and can be somewhat introverted. Very realistic, and with great powers of concentration, you relate best to those well known to you but are cautious with strangers. Your emotions are controlled and self-discipline is strongly in evidence. You are contemplative and reflective. You approach life intellectually, and with great attention to detail. You may show considerable executive ability but often need the leadership qualities shown by the large handwriter to put your ideas to maximum effect. You can be quite independent of what others think.

In business Your capacity for accuracy and aptitude, for detailed, scientific work makes you invaluable, as does your ability to work alone for long periods of time on a project. You also work extremely well in areas where confidentiality and loyalty are important. You will always exhibit a very well-developed sense of economy.

As a lover Not overly imaginative but tender and thoughtful, you have a strong tendency to discipline impulses and emotions, so a sensual and loving partner can be of immense help to your controlled personality. Loyalty rates highly, so you rarely run off with the lover of your best friend! As a small writer, you loathe your partner giving away intimate details of your personal relationship, so your partner will have to learn not to discuss you with others. You also frown on public displays of affection. Small, well-chosen gifts are the order of the day for you.

As a parent Praising your offspring does not come naturally to you, since you can often feel overrated yourself when given genuine praise and believe the same applies to your children. You do not like parting with your money, so you won't necessarily provide designer jeans or trainers, unless of course they will last for many years. However, you will invariably provide money for whatever you consider wise and of long-term benefit to your offspring, such as exchange visits with other students. You encourage academic pursuits and exude a quiet air of approval – sometimes!

VARYING

I am not in a good mood
But I might be better later
Hope So

You can be very charming but also very erratic – one day full of ideas, the next day unimaginative, dull and boring. Frequently you exhibit childish behaviour and may often feel off-balance, both personally and professionally. You long for success one moment and welcome the mundane the next. You can be very talkative one moment and silent the next. Your dominant traits will be self-centredness and moodiness.

In business There is a strong tendency to drive those around you to distraction. You will praise their ideas one moment and deny they even made a suggestion the next; worse still, you may even claim someone else's brilliant idea as your own. Very difficult to pin down to a particular course of action, you are likely to change arrangements at the last moment. Your intermittent charm and great sense of humour rarely compensate for your mood swings and inconsistency.

As a lover Your lover may swing from the chandelier tonight and go unnoticed tomorrow: 'I will always love you' and 'What are you hanging around for?' are alternate responses you are likely to offer them. You will provide excitement, you will cause tears and above all, you will offer uncertainty: giving your lover a diamond ring today and forgetting that all-important anniversary tomorrow. Your lover will need a lot of patience to deal with you!

As a parent Bouts of absolute adoration and praise for your children are followed by frustration: 'The children are getting under my feet, can't you control them?' You need a very stable partner, one who will make up for the times that you fail to meet promises or obligations. At times, you will ply your children with wonderful, expensive gifts, but these can be inappropriate and to your liking rather than your children's. Although undisciplined, you are also very entertaining and amusing, younger children tend to adore you and see only what is good. As they mature, they may well wonder whether you were always so unreliable.

2

Zone Sizes

balanced zones

dominant upper ←

dominant middle ←

dominant lower zone ←

BALANCED

act of writing — 1.
Thought I would to
clear, but trying s
I fuss about havin

If you stick to the copybook proportions, you have a balanced outlook, with an equal focus on the three dominant areas: intellectual, social and instinctual. You are a happy person with inner harmony. There is no exaggerated trait, and you generally progress through life with a contented attitude and wholesome self-confidence.

In business As you rarely over- or underestimate your own abilities, you tend to find employment that will neither push you beyond your abilities nor hold you back. You believe in fair pay for a good day's work and will resist anyone taking advantage of you. Fairness, loyalty and reliability are all characteristic of you as a worker. You may not set the world alight, but you won't be lost in the crowd. You will fight for the rights of your fellow-workers and would make a good union leader or supervisor. Your energy level is good and you pace yourself very well indeed.

As a lover Your partner and family mean a great deal to you, and you give the same attention to your family responsibilities that you do to your business commitments. You like a well-kept home and are quite happy to help with the household tasks. Fairness rates very highly with you and you are more than happy to 'pull your weight'. You are a good provider and are very loyal to your partner. A good standard of living is important to you, and you enjoy luxuries but do not need them. Sexually, you are considerate and active.

As a parent You are the nice, solid type who enjoys family life. You praise and encourage your children when appropriate but also insist that they make their contribution, whether it be helping with the housework, doing their share of the cooking or eventually contributing to the expenses. You encourage your children to grow, develop and become responsible adults, and you promote a healthy environment.

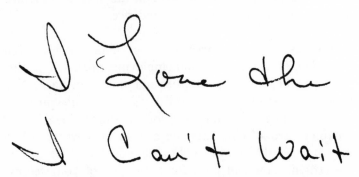

Basically, your interests are of an intellectual and possibly spiritual nature. You are a person with high ideals and aspirations but little interest in everyday commitments. There are no solid foundations to your personality and your endeavours may not be rooted in reality. Your active imagination is allied to idealism and the tendency to daydream. Often very well-read, with an interest in all the arts, you can be insufficiently down-to-earth to know what you really want from life.

In business   A 'good-ideas' person, you need the help of colleagues for your ideas to reach fruition. You show a lot of ambition, but become very disillusioned when others do not reach the high standards you consider acceptable. You are very proud and take offence quite easily. You can be very critical of yourself and others and are not the most cheerful person to work with. Under pressure you tend to flee to your active dream life.

As a lover   You will take your lover to concerts, the theatre and movies but will be very critical of what you see. As your feet are not firmly on the ground, you can mislead your partner as to your earning capacity, status in society, and so on, so don't be surprised if others don't believe everything they are told! With your uncompromising ideas of what is right and what is wrong, you are easily upset, so others must be on their best behaviour at all times. You are not very cheerful and things must be just right to put you in a sexual frame of mind. Although you have a good imagination, you are always frightened of doing the 'wrong' thing sexually.

As a parent   Strict and uncompromising, you expect your children to do their very best at all times, and you will be very disappointed if they do not attain top grades in all their subjects. You are not tactile, so children can feel unloved unless their other parent is warm and affectionate. You show little interest in the children's social life and will discourage much interaction with friends and neighbours. You lack a sense of humour.

DOMINANT MIDDLE ZONE

for your helpful
I'm looking forward
handwriting samples!

You live for today – what is happening now is what is important – and you are very self-involved. Teenagers, who think of nothing more than their own daily activities, commonly exhibit this writing style. Often strong-willed and self-reliant, with a big ego, you want excitement on a daily basis and have difficulty in delaying pleasure. You can be most inconsiderate of the needs of others but seem completely unaware of it. Your conceit can be great and you can make a big deal of trivia.

In business   You frequently want to be the leader and you do have some leadership qualities, but you tell others what to do rather than ask, and want things done your way. Your presumptuousness is very difficult to handle and you tend to antagonize those who work with you. At times you are lazy and can indulge yourself in taking time off for minor reasons.

As a lover A lover may arrive on your doorstep and literally be dragged to the bedroom, since you have difficulty delaying pleasure. You can be hard to satisfy, and repeat performances may be the order of the day. You can also be quite generous, but the whole world will know about it. You welcome and encourage your partners to spend money on you. You can overindulge in eating, drinking and clothes-buying.

As a parent As you are very wrapped up in your own needs you can find great difficulty in handling the needs of a child. However, you will, when it suits you, overindulge them too. You will line up a good array of baby-sitters, friends and relations to help with your children when your own needs take priority. Invariably, you love your kids and will buy them the best and send them to expensive schools, but you are sometimes emotionally unavailable to them.

DOMINANT LOWER ZONE

a little gmb
round my tummy
a honey pot

Sex, money and sporting interests are what matter to you. You have tremendous physical energy but find it difficult to channel it into productive outlets. At times you will be totally driven by ideas for making money (often quick ways) while at other times you will leave the office at lunch-time to play a round of golf. You may need more than one outlet for your sexual energy or, at best, wear out your partner with your sexual demands. Frequently, your type has many creative ideas but often needs help in carrying them out. Sometimes you are over-emotional.

In business You are an exciting, exuberant go-getter, but so variable! You may run your own business (hopefully with a small handwriter!) where you do not have to answer to others for your erratic behaviour. When you do push to close a deal, no one will show more energy and drive, particularly when the rewards are very high. But on a day when you do not feel like being in the office, you might as well forget it. You are whimsical, may lack maturity, but you are also charming, and can reach great heights of success, even if you fall flat on your face a number of times *en route*! You are a bad timekeeper and one of your favourite sayings is 'the cheque is in the post'.

As a lover Above all, you are demanding and like variety. You want all the good things in life: expensive restaurants, being seen in the best holiday spots with a sexy, very attractive partner in tow, fast cars, designer labels, a detached home (preferably with a swimming pool and space for four cars). You often live above your means but do not feel too much guilt about this. Life for your lover will never be boring, but it can be worrying. You just might abandon your partner for one of their beautiful friends!

As a parent You may be quite doting, but you won't always keep your promises. In due time your children will get what they want, but as and when it is convenient for you. You love showing off your children and will ensure that they always look wonderful. The children will also flaunt designer labels and the latest toys; what they often miss out on is time and attention, which can come at a premium with you and compete with your other activities.

3

Slant

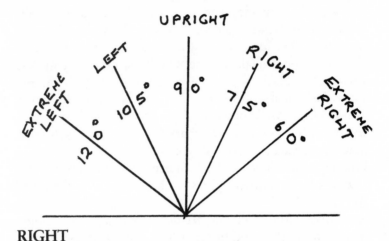

UPRIGHT

LEFT

RIGHT

EXTREME LEFT

EXTREME RIGHT

120°

105°

90°

75°

60°

RIGHT

Such a beautiful cruise.
Such a pretty lady!
Tomorrow Gibralter!!

You have a friendly, affectionate nature, capable of communicating feelings and ideas to others. You are emotionally responsive and demonstrative, and look to the future with positive ideas. You respond to others in a sympathetic manner and experience no difficulty in getting along with them. You have a genuine social quality, enjoy entertaining others and being entertained by them. You tend to hold on to friends for many years and are at your best when surrounded by other people. You are a very progressive thinker. You dislike long periods of time alone.

In business The ability to communicate easily and well tends to draw your type towards sales and marketing positions, or any position where direct contact is a strong requirement. You love forward planning in everything and can become restless if you have nothing new and demanding to look forward to. You work hard and enthusiastically.

As a lover You are delightful, charming, romantic, caring and easy to get along with. Your affectionate personality enables you to attract others easily. A good and active social life is necessary, both in and outside the home. You are capable of warmth and variety in your sex life, and you readily give unexpected gifts and perform acts of kindness.

As a parent Again, you are caring, demonstrative and communicative, always ready with a listening ear and prepared to encourage and praise your offspring. You look on life as one big adventure and encourage your children to do likewise. Enquiring, enterprising and enthusiastic, you consider anything and everything worth sharing; for you it is paramount that the family enjoy things together in a good family environment.

EXTREME RIGHT

I have pleasure in enclosing a cheque of premium paid in respect of the

Over the top! You are constantly crying or laughing, very impulsive and in need of constant change and variety. You are terribly enthusiastic about new ideas and always dashing from one to the other, without understanding why

25

others are more controlled. You can miss out on the good things of today for the dreams of tomorrow. You do communicate but your listener must have a lot of time to spare as you do not know when to stop your 'ear-bashing'. You can become hysterical under pressure and may wear yourself out at an early age.

In business Too rash by far, you need a really tight rein to keep you steady. You tend to move on to new ideas before getting the maximum out of existing ones. Impatient with colleagues and customers, you will exaggerate stories beyond all recognition. Yours is a theatrical personality and you join causes on impulse. You can make an extremely successful salesperson, but others won't be able to believe all you tell them!

As a lover You are the 'head over heels at first sight' type, and you require undivided attention at all times. You are very demonstrative anywhere, but you also tend to be extremely jealous and possessive. You must be fed on large doses of charm, flattery and sex. You hate being left alone even for reasonably short periods of time, for you consider this neglect, and can behave in a quite resentful fashion. Your romantic impulses are ardent, demanding and overpowering; this can be flattering initially, but difficult to cope with over the long run.

As a parent 'My child is the best', 'My child does not tell lies' – sound familiar? Everything about your children is beyond criticism in public and it is very difficult for children in this situation to get a balanced view of what is good or bad, right or wrong. At other times you go to the other extreme and punish the child excessively for actual or imagined misdemeanours within the home. It is important to you to project an image of the 'perfect' family, and you display group family photos around your home. You are too extreme to come anywhere close to a model parent.

Now is the time
to the aid of th
The quick brow
jumped over the t

This example shows a balance between the mind and the emotions. Your character is generally reserved, with a dry sense of humour. Your responses are cautious, considered and to-the-point. You have the ability to accept the responsibilities of life and regard them with a dedicated calmness. You have a very independent personality and would make a good planner or organizer. At times you may appear cold, calculating and sceptical. You are loyal, honest, self-controlled and live in the present moment.

In business Your loyalty and self-reliance are without question the most entrenched of all the personality-types. Likewise, your impartial attitudes and independent thinking can be invaluable. You can make an excellent leader or equally contented loner, and your ability to remain calm when everything is falling down around you is unequalled. However, you loathe criticism and will give up on a task if anyone suggests that you are unable to carry it out properly.

As a lover You show your loyalty with everyday acts of kindness and consideration. Your emotions are kept in check and you take a long time to give your total commitment. But once committed, you hang on to what is dear to you for life. Fickleness is not a feature of your personality type and you welcome the responsibility of home life. In arguing a point, you will appeal to logic rather than emotion. You are a good, solid, steadfast lover – perhaps not the most romantic but the most sustaining. You always remember birthdays and anniversaries, and tend to give practical gifts.

As a parent You enjoy the responsibilities and joys of family life, so take to it easily. You give praise where praise is due and encourage, or even criticize where necessary. You can be a very caring parent who will take the time and trouble to explain things to your offspring. You are likely to make outings to museums and art galleries, and will not spoil or overinduldge. You encourage your children to think for themselves and make decisions independently. Kisses and affection are not abundant but are given spontaneously when required.

LEFT

relevant off-the-job train
It is important that each
co-ordinated and it is su
Agent' he is responsible
Financial support to emplo'

Your two most dominant traits are caution and sensitivity. You can be quite passive and may even display defensive and negative attitudes, but once you overcome your initial caution, you move forward with much determination. Sensitivity does play a big part in how much risk-taking you will consider. You fear ridicule and tend to hide your emotions, possibly displaying a well-constructed front to cover up and compensate for inner feelings of withdrawal. You often repress feelings and can become very anxious and fearful in new situations. As a left-slanter you tend to resist change or progress and will stay in the same job for many years rather than risk the challenge of a new environment. (In many cases of left-slanting handwriting, the mother has played a dominant role and the positive male identification is jeopardized.) However, there are many highly successful left-slanters who learn eventually to cut from their past and, although they will never be as relaxed as right-slanters, they do adapt.

In business You would make a very good historian, or excel in a job that involves research or anything relating to the past, such as antique-collecting or dealing. You can be very self-centred and selfish, and thus experience some difficulty in getting along with others. You may seek a position of a solitary nature and can work very well when on your own.

As a lover Slow and cautious, you may be the sort to marry late in life, but if you do give your affections to another you are theirs for life. You need constant reassurance that you are the one and only and can be very selfish in your demands for affection. However, you seldom return these displays of affection and can leave a partner feeling frustrated and angry. You may have had a very close relationship with your mother (or mother-figure), and may well take her on holiday or on shopping expeditions; you need a tolerant partner. You generally don't mix well and prefer the company of those close to you or a small circle of friends.

As a parent Your caution rises strongly to the surface, and you want your children to do *safe* things – take safe jobs and stay close to home. Praise doesn't come easy but criticism does. You will always say 'it is for your own good', but this can be extremely difficult to take and lead to shy, secretive and retiring offspring. You also worry unnecessarily about the health of your children, taking preventative measures which may be unwarranted.

EXTREME LEFT

extreme Left is rarely found and suggests extreme caution in everything one does.

This slant appears very rarely, and the traits described above will apply but heightened to the extreme.

MIXED (right, left and upright)

During my training I became a hairdresser. Finally I gave up.

This is a fascinating script, and surprisingly common. You are subject to swinging moods: happy one minute, dejected and lonely the next. Everything about you is inconsistent and unsettled; your intellect and emotions are in constant conflict – the mind wants to do one thing, the heart another. Common sense and good judgement are lacking and you can become very excitable over trivia. On the positive side, you are always interesting and provocative, and seem to have an inborn ability to relate to many types of personalities.

In business The inconsistency can cause problems and

certainly you experience difficulty in dealing with superiors. You become very nervous and anxious when dealing with people you consider more intelligent than yourself, but in dealing with others who have problems, you come into your own and can be extremely helpful. You can feel socially inferior and off-centre, and often long for a position of responsibility where you will do your utmost to control your capricious nature. My experience has shown that this type often work brilliantly as prison wardens, probation officers and traffic wardens.

As a lover You can be difficult: warm and ardent one moment, cold the next, constantly in need of reassurance, yet doubting that you are worthy of such love. Your emotional nature is so erratic that others never know how you will react to them. You are probably the most difficult partner of all – highly sexed one moment, and completely disinterested at other times. You might walk out at any time and leave your lover for another, but then be surprised if you are not welcomed back with open arms!

As a parent You are not sufficiently consistent in your expressions of love and affection. Children will tend to feel insecure in this environment and wonder if they are to blame for the frequent mood changes; sensitive children may feel inferior and lack confidence. This is a clear case for seeking aid with parenting skills. You are not guilty of unkindness, just inadequate in maintaining the consistency from which most children benefit.

4

Baseline

STRAIGHT

RIGID

VERY   UNEVEN

RISING

FALLING

STRAIGHT

A very Happy Christmas + a happy new Year.

Your script indicates stability; you are not easily upset. Your mind disciplines your emotions and you are not easily swayed by every little event or the expressed thoughts of others. You demonstrate orderliness and dependability.

In business You get your priorities right and are not distracted by events going on around you. You organize yourself well and adhere to all promises, deadlines and commitments. You behave in a very stable manner and are happy to assist others who may ask for your help, or time. You demonstrate emotional stability at all levels.

As a lover You always follow through with any plans made, and you feel extremely uncomfortable if you have to let anyone down, even for a very justifiable reason. If someone has a problem, you are an excellent listener and frequently come up with sound, sensible advice. You are a very caring lover, with as much desire to please as to be pleased.

As a parent You are utterly reliable and will stick to any promise made to your offspring. You need an orderly environment and will not tolerate untidiness or slovenly ways so your children will be expected to do their homework at the right time and keep their areas clean and tidy. You will, however, always be there for them to assist in whatever ways are necessary, and you are flexible in your approach to each of your children.

EXCESSIVELY RIGID

become a Hairdresser. Dunr training I have been undecic wether that it was the ngt career for me. Finally in n third uear I have decided this

Your writing shows a desire for control; you may lose your spontaneity and behave in an inhibited manner. You drain your energy through the fear of ever letting others know what you are really like. You may have had a parent who expected you to be 'seen but not heard'. When you do lose your cool, all hell breaks loose, but these times are few and far between.

In business You tend to choose your jobs very carefully and avoid situations where you are greatly exposed to others, or expected to work in a team situation. Always at the back of your mind is the thought: 'They will find out I am not as clever as I claim to be', or 'They just won't like me.' You also greatly fear emotional outbursts, both from yourself and from others.

As a lover You are too inhibited and self-conscious to relax and enjoy the great pleasures that a satisfactory, close sexual relationship can bring. You worry about how you look without your clothes. 'Are my breasts too small/large?' 'Is my penis too small? Will I get an erection?' Very occasionally you say 'sod-it' and have a ball! Once every five years, maybe!

As a parent You restrict your offspring greatly and are frightened of every fresh move they make. They are rarely allowed to travel far from home or spend the night with their school friends. You will teach them to save their pocket-money for a rainy day and behave cautiously in everything they do. You are a kindly parent but very restrictive.

VERY UNEVEN

1. feel that my bones are beginning to ache. and all this psychopathical statement has been no good.

You are basically unreliable and lacking in will-power. You make all sorts of promises that you know you cannot keep. Clever and capable, you may nevertheless fail at a job for which you are highly suited. Others will wonder why, but it is because of your inability to apply yourself and your difficulty in sticking to a routine. This applies equally to your hobbies and interests. You can be extremely emotional and, at times, confused.

In business Your lack of reliability often leads to frequent job changes and discontent. You are an erratic timekeeper and an inconsistent problem-solver. You are a victim of your own wavering moods, and although you can be very cheerful and friendly, others do tire of your unpredictability and mood swings.

As a lover Sometimes you are attentive and demonstrative; at other times you show disinterest in everything about you. Sex can be a joy or a disaster. You may shower a lover with gifts one day and borrow money from them the next. You may love and loathe them all at the same time. Even friendships that are soundly based on common interests can become strained because of your fluctuating moods.

As a parent You are just as variable towards your children as you are towards your lover. One day you will play with them and take an interest in them; at other times you may ignore them and insist they stay out of your way. You will overspend on them sometimes and fail to provide them with necessary money at other times. You will make them promises that you have no hope of fulfilling. It is vital to have one reliable partner in this situation.

RISING

Please be Kind to me had a very trying day

35

Your script is a very positive one, which shows that you are optimistic and not easily discouraged. You maintain a hopeful attitude and are genuinely happy in whatever you are doing. You make a very cheery companion and are usually willing to lend a helping hand. You express positive attitudes as well as the desire to succeed. You can, however, be restless and over-excitable at times. You don't enjoy too much routine, but should someone suggest something new and interesting to you, you will quickly stir to action. If the rise is exaggerated, it indicates that too much energy is being expended too widely.

In business You are a go-getter who faces problems head on, a pleasant person who sees life as a challenge. You show cheerfulness in the face of adversity and are invariably positive in everything you undertake. Ambitious, you do not expect everything to be given to you on a plate, and you strive with enthusiasm and a buoyant spirit. On the negative side, your organizational ability can be impaired due to your impatience. Good advice might be to slow down and keep your feet more firmly on the ground.

As a lover You would make a charming companion or lover. More often than not, you are in a good mood or, at least, looking on the bright side. You experience no difficulty in adapting yourself socially and will show consideration, generosity, and pride in your partner. Sexually you are inventive and always a lot of fun. You love treating your partner as special and will choose very thoughtful gifts not just for birthdays or special occasions but at any time.

As a parent Happy, cheerful, bright and encouraging, you will get involved with school committees, sports-day organization, etc. You feel pride and joy in your offspring and are capable of making a very happy home life, where children prosper and produce their best efforts. You will encourage your children to try and try again and any lack of success will not be frowned upon. They will be encouraged to try new and different things until they find something they are good at.

FALLING

This script reveals a pessimistic attitude. You do not become enthusiastic about new ideas and are likely to be sceptical of others who do. You lack drive, initiative and the desire to get pleasure from life, preferring to complain and always adopting negative attitudes. You seem to thrive on disparaging remarks, such as, 'The hot weather kills me' or 'Won't be long till winter's here and we'll all freeze to death!' There is no pleasing you.

In business You may well be very good in your chosen profession, but your type are rarely popular. You nit-pick and tend to blame others if things go wrong, imagining slights and rejection and frequently putting off till tomorrow what could easily be done today. Even when you are praised you feel unworthy, and often cover this up under an arrogant exterior. You may give in before you even try a particular task.

As a lover 'I'm not in the mood tonight, perhaps I shall feel more like it tomorrow' or 'I think I have a headache coming on' – these responses are typical of you. You can easily dampen a lover's ardour and enthusiasm by discussing all your problems, real or imagined, at the wrong moment, leaving them feeling tired and depressed. When others buy you gifts, you immediately suspect that they will be unsuitable, inappropriate or just the wrong colour.

As a parent Your negative attitudes tend to hold your children back in many areas. You may discourage their participation in sports-day events or advise them before a competition that they 'haven't a chance of winning'. Invariably you consider their teachers too modern or too old-fashioned; too strict or too lenient – never just right. One of the commonest remarks in your household could be 'In my day, we didn't ask for money, we went out and earned it'. You are prone to expect too much from your children and to give too little. There is much too much criticism in your household and not enough encouragement.

5

Connectedness/
Disconnectedness

Connected The majority of the letters are joined. Allowance can be made for breaks after capitals and other very occasional breaks.

Connected

Disconnected This writing shows only four letters in a word, or less, written with one continuous stroke.

Disconnected

TOTALLY DISCONNECTED

WORDS SOMETIMES Connected

CONNECTED

simultaneously   with   the

building   and   including

into   a   revised   total ?

You know from the beginning of any project just what you are going to do from start to finish. Your thinking is systematic and logical, and you are normally practical and realistic. You don't trust intuition, and analyse everything. You become very restless if your mind is not constantly stimulated, and you often feel more relaxed doing a crossword, or any puzzle, rather than doing nothing. Personal problems are difficult for you as you are much better at solving abstract ones. You can be very tactless. There are times when you are so busy thinking about what happened yesterday, or what will happen tomorrow, that you miss the pleasures today has to offer.

In business You have a great capacity for getting things done – but woe betide anyone who interrupts you *en route*: you will cooperate when you have reached a proper stopping point, but only then. You are a good organizer and plan ahead well. You rarely jump to conclusions without first stopping to reason things out, but you can sometimes get bogged down by detail, be pedantic, nit-picking and too self-involved.

As a lover On the whole, you are very sentimental but can lack empathy, unless it is with an ailment you have experienced, e.g., headache or backache; any unfamiliar ailment will quite readily be dismissed. At times you take things too literally and can thus get hurt quite easily. You will, however, hide these feelings, and this can be confusing for your lover. You have a very good memory for what you consider essentials, but day-to-day obligations (taking your partner out to dinner, or to a doctor) can be forgotten, so it is a good idea, perhaps even a necessity, to write these things down. You are not the most imaginative lover but you have good staying power!

As a parent You were, or are, probably a good student, who enjoys reading and study, and you will expect the same from your offspring. You may be disappointed if your children are less academic than you were, and creative and sporting skills will not be given the notice or praise they deserve. However, you are a caring person and communicate well when approached at the right time. You do not inspire confidence.

DISCONNECTED

Jo wish You a very happy Christmas an a New Year.

You are very intuitive and show an unusual insight into the minds and motives of other people. You react on first meeting with either approval or disapproval, rarely changing your mind at a later date. You are very individualistic and are often fascinated by the unusual – that is, as long as the idea appeals. As you tend to have a 'grasshopper' mind, your interests and ideas can change quite readily. Normally, your type are collectors of rare and unusual objects. Emotionally, you are sensitive and need time alone to protect yourself from over-stimulation. But you can be moody, restless, antisocial, selfish, and very critical of others, without much insight into your own moods and motives.

In business Your critical faculty can be very useful, and you would make a very good theatre or film critic. Keen observation and a great memory for impressions are two of your talents. You have great imaginative potential, inspirational and innovative thoughts and ideas; you may enjoy writing stories and poetry. Your instinctual reactions can result in violent, verbal outbursts, making it difficult for you to work in a team but, left to your own devices, you can produce ideas or works of great originality. At other times, you may demonstrate an erratic kind of thinking that leads nowhere.

As a lover You're original, lively and imaginative if your lover is in favour; but otherwise totally disinterested. Your

41

desires vary from feelings of tender love to just plain lust. You can be turned on by a moonlight walk or walking in the mud, and are provocative and stimulating. You are a great animal lover too and may invite Rufus (the dog) or Sam (the cat) to share the bed with you. You want material possessions, but do not need them. You may offer your lover instead the first daffodil of spring, a beautifully coloured stone from the beach, or even a poem written especially for them. Are you prepared to go backpacking in outer Mongolia to see the apes? If you are the stay-at-home type, avoid the disconnected writer; they will not settle for the mundane. Despite their somewhat selfish natures, these people attract others from all walks of life and are rarely short of friends. Nice to have around.

As a parent You take an interest in everything the children have to say and do: yours is the household where the children's drawings are hung all over the fridge door and possibly up the staircase as well. Conker-collecting, nature rambles, picnicking and camping could all be part of their upbringing, and family pets will feature strongly. Each child in this household will be treated as an individual and their strengths and weaknesses handled accordingly.

TOTALLY DISCONNECTED (cursive or print)

You have difficulty in understanding yourself and other people. You may be introverted and have feelings of inadequacy, a loner who can be both competitive and rebellious. You tend to have a dislike of authority figures, and normal rules and regulations. Your reactions are instinctive and you are very quick to jump to conclusions. Always critical and aloof, you experience great difficulty in linking experiences to meaningful direction. You can be inconsistent in your behavioural patterns, and behave in an immature manner. Invariably, your type is very self-centred.

In business You will be competitive in whatever you decide to work at, but you much prefer to work alone and unsupervised. You strive for perfection and are often disappointed that you do not attain the high standards you set for yourself. You like to work when you feel like it, rather than be committed to specific times. You are likely to be particularly good at working with your hands and would make a superb carpenter, builder, mechanical engineer or decorator.

As a lover You share time with your partner as and when you want to, and quite often choose to be alone. Though you feel quite empty at times, you rarely admit this to those who care for you. Basically, you are not co-operative, and are mean with social overtures. At times your antisocial behaviour is such that your partner will feel more comfortable socializing alone, as you are unaware of your unreasonable behaviour. Sexually, you need ego-boosting and confirmation that you are the best, the one and only. Trust does not come high on your list of character traits.

As a parent You are inconsistent, wavering between showing a lot of care and not being around because you are following your own pursuits. As you loathe being tied down or committed, any limitations the children impose, such as the need for babysitters, will irritate and receive little consideration. You find it difficult, not to say impossible to adapt your behaviour to suit a situation and have a complicated and strained relationship with your partner and your children.

WORDS SOMETIMES CONNECTED

it says I am a ought not to find it

You have an avant-garde type of creativity and originality. You are exacting in your business transactions but have blind spots in your concentration. You see openings and opportunities that others miss, but can be careless about detail. You possess intense mental energy, love completing crosswords and studying languages; you may have an interest in creative writing. You also enjoy many cultural interests, such as art, literature and music.

6

Letter Shapes

m	ᜫᜫᜫᜫᜫᜫᜫ	ARCADE
ω	‿‿‿‿‿‿‿	GARLAND
M	⋀⋀⋀⋀⋀	ANGULAR
ᜄ	‿⌢‿‿‿	THREAD
ᜋ	∞∞∞∞∞∞∞	ROUNDED

ARCADE

I am 18 years old and f
the past 2½ years, since lea
school I have been training t

You are slow to accept change unless it is gradual, a traditionalist who is very protective of everything. Screening your thoughts and bottling your feelings comes naturally to you. You tend to shut out the outside world and have a strong dislike of consulting others about what you consider to be your business. You treat your home as a place of security from the outside world and can be overly secretive. You are a serious person who takes a long time to make a decision but adheres strictly to it once made.

In business Your perseverance may lead to your becoming head of an organization. You can be slow to learn but once something is learned, it is never forgotten. You are very fair, and could well be a talented public speaker.

45

You don't allow anyone to dominate you, and you get along well with most people, but on the whole you are reserved and can be somewhat sceptical. Many of your type display an artistic sense of proportion and can be creative in a practical sense. Your emotions are well controlled.

As a lover Though you are quite warm and affectionate, you don't often show it, either emotionally or sexually. You are very loyal to those you trust but it can take a long time for you to commit to a long-term relationship. You appreciate quality paintings, sculptures and handcrafted articles. You show good taste and will invest in items expected to increase in value. You may be musically talented or, at least, show great appreciation of music. You are in no way given to fickleness and tend to remain with partners for life.

As a parent Naturally reserved, you do not like your children to discuss your business away from home. You enjoy the security of married life and welcome a few, well-chosen friends to your home. Your children will probably have a small circle of friends, whom you have approved. They will be encouraged to work hard to achieve their full potential. Over-indulgence is not likely to feature, either emotionally or materially, but a good standard of education will be a goal, with university or technical training if appropriate.

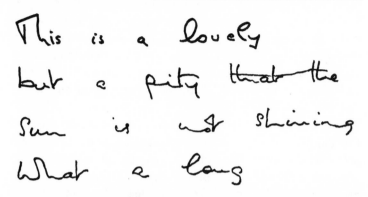

You are the easy-going type, and invariably remain pleasant and obliging. Generally you are passive and try hard to avoid arguments or confrontation. You adapt easily to changes in circumstance and are very sensitive to atmosphere. You are at your happiest when entertaining in your own home and make an excellent host or hostess. It is very important to you to be accepted by others and you can actually go overboard in your attempt to be liked. Genuine niceness, kind-heartedness and charm, together with a sympathetic disposition, all go to make you a particularly pleasing individual.

In business You may have considerable ability in your chosen career (check other writing movements), but your motto is: 'Be nice to everyone on the way up; you just might meet them on the way down'. Some of your type have particular ability in jobs relating to the worlds of art and literature. You are extremely approachable and will always be prepared to listen to others' viewpoints. However, others would be ill-advised to pick a quarrel with you – you will literally run, or take to your sickbed, until things return to normal.

As a lover Open, warm, and receptive, with a responsive nature, you treat your partner with affection and thoroughly enjoy the lover/husband/wife role. Nothing gives you greater pleasure than to be surrounded by your loved ones, at family parties, weddings, christenings – and you will always be prepared to do all the catering. Romance and thoughtfulness are part of your overall character. So if someone wants flowers regularly, or return visits to special places, you would be an ideal partner for them.

As a parent You are loving and caring but too passive; the children tend to run rings around you. They soon learn to do what they like, knowing full well that you will not confront them or do anything that will lead to arguments in the home. You may leave too many things unsaid, so that your children cannot easily recognize their boundaries. However, since you and your husband or wife will invariably have a very happy life together after your offspring have 'flown the nest', your children will always be welcomed home. You are the type to feel very disappointed if your children cannot be around you at Christmas or on your birthday. You will make an excellent grandparent.

ANGULAR

believe is your change for a full report. I don't have any specific questions to ask, & unfortunately can't provide an earlier sample.

Determined and competitive, you thrive on hard work and problem-solving. You can be inflexible, but show a high degree of maturity and mental energy. Nothing delights you more than being in command and on top of a situation. You demonstrate independence of spirit as well as the ability to keep your emotions under control. You make a good leader but have great difficulty with any form of compromise. You have an aptitude for thoroughness and practical application, and you are idealistic, with a probing mind that wants answers, even to the inexplicable. You can be very sarcastic.

In business You are positive, ambitious and work extremely hard to achieve your aims. Such is your determination that you will invariably reach the top of your profession. Some might call you hard, and you certainly set high standards, both for yourself and for others. You have limited patience for waffling and petty excuses and expect others to come straight to the point. A great individualist, you know what you want and how to get it. You are self-critical, analytical and logical, with a love of computers.

As a lover Human emotion baffles you, so a lover's appeals to you must be based on logic. You save your affection for your partner rather than for the children, home or family pet. Often you appear reserved, but can be possessive and jealous. If you encounter any major problems in a relationship, you will make every effort to sort it out, but you can't be bothered with trivial problems, such as the broken-down washer or vacuum cleaner! You can be a very aggressive lover and quite imaginative, but, at times, you may appear cold, indifferent or preoccupied. The most up-to-date piece of technological equipment is a prized gift here.

As a parent Encouraging but tough, you adopt an air of control and discipline which pervade the household. You do not like the children staying in bed late or sitting around doing nothing; instead you encourage activity – game-playing or sports. You welcome questions and will do your best to answer them truthfully. On the whole, you are a good parent, if perhaps a little strict at times. You encourage job-taking during holidays and show a great deal of pride in academic success.

Today we are at sea having
Spent two very hectic days in
Leningrad.

Normally you are diplomatic and mix very well with all types of personalities. You dislike arguments and solve problems by compromise rather than argument. Adaptability, versatility and impressionability are all characteristics of yours, though you can be evasive and deceitful. You don't like being limited to a particular course of action and if you are, you are likely to make a number of changes *en route*. Your writing shows high intelligence and a love of the arts. Socially you can be inconsiderate and difficult to understand. Your concentration is often divided and you are susceptible to influences from others. Favouring appreciation rather than material gain, yours is a highly interesting type.

In business As tact and diplomacy are strong traits, you can be very useful to have around, but there is no guarantee that you will be around when others need you. However, you are extremely charming and often sublimate your own creative talents in order to bring them out in others. Your ideas are original and your intellect keen. You may be a lecturer, a teacher, or work in a charitable capacity. Broadminded, you rarely frown on anyone.

As a lover You are really quite charming, tender and loving, but not always as truthful or reliable as one might wish – you may well change appointments, or arrangements, at the last moment. You have a wide variety of changing interests, and are happy to include those close to you in your outings. You are curious about a great many things, and a love of art comes high on your list as do wining, dining and exotic foods. You give colourful descriptions of places you have visited and can transport listeners with your descriptive tales. It is easy for others to forgive you for many of your weaknesses, as your positive traits compensate for so much.

As a parent You may spoil your children but you also open their minds to many things. You listen to their ideas, encourage and praise their endeavours and intuitively know how to handle the different personalities within the household. At times, you do not make yourself available to do things when promised, but you try to compensate by arranging exciting outings. Your ideas are as numerous as your mind is open.

ROUNDED

close an addvessed
k and hope that you
ply if you are not to

It is considered unusual for an adult to write in this way but perfectly normal for a teenager. Immaturity is shown, as is the need for reassurance. Not a good decision-maker, you tend to discuss your problems with all your friends before reaching a conclusion – then you are likely to change the decision, again and again. You can be very emotional and go overboard for very minor reasons. Jealousy and possessiveness are frequently close to the surface, and you may create scenes in public. You have a great desire for security, yet find it difficult, whatever the circumstances, to feel secure. Constant reassurance is needed here, and others do tire of your demands.

In business   You can be very lazy and self-indulgent, working when you want to but finding all sorts of excuses for not completing a certain task or project. It is never your fault: 'The figures weren't available' or 'The computer isn't working properly' – anything to save your skin. You are very childish. Fortunately, very few adults write with a totally rounded script.

As a lover   'How many times have I told you I love you?' could well be your partner's most frequent remark. Sexually you are very eager, but then self-doubt settles upon you again. You are very kind, and would give a lover everything you own, but you want to own them too – you want their heart, mind, soul and body, and that can be very difficult for your lover to handle. This is expected, perhaps, at 15 – but not when we reach our adult life. You may love showering gifts on your lover, but again, it is because you are seeking approval. You can become very upset and emotional if your lover forgets to acknowledge your birthday or anniversary.

As a parent   You over-indulge them – almost like a child caring for children. You are very protective towards them and will fight anyone who threatens the security of any family member, but, in all other ways you prefer compromise to argument. Your children will be beautifully dressed and fed whatever they desire, but little discipline will be exercised. Rarely will they be denied the latest toys or clothes. Of course, this makes them brattish. It is too important for you to keep up with the Joneses.

7

Writing Styles

Simplified

Original

Loopy

Ornate

SIMPLIFIED

sleeping area.

.... and it was

so that the new bedroom

down to the lower tier

You like a direct approach to everything and strive to simplify issues. You may be highly intelligent but you can also be very impatient. You have a quick grasp and assimilation of essentials, a bias towards reserve, discretion and matter-of-factness. As you invariably have a high degree of energy and a very quick mind you are capable of reaching great heights. However, you do not like others to disagree with you and make a poor listener. You are disciplined and a great go-getter.

In business You show many leadership qualities and are probably (or will be) at the top of your chosen profession. Capable of easily distinguishing the important from the unimportant, you work at a great speed. You are a happy mixture of imagination and intelligence which enables you to make your dreams come true. You can be intolerant of others who do not grasp facts as quickly as you do and they will be left in no doubt as to how you feel about them, for you will say it straight to their face! You admire achievement and will encourage those you consider deserving of your time and energy.

As a lover Without an intelligent partner, you will soon be bored to tears. Cocktail parties have no appeal as you cannot tolerate small talk, but invite some academics, writers, artists, or others at the top of their field, around for dinner and you will be in your element. Your directness can get you into trouble socially, as you speak your mind much too readily. Sexually you are active but have a fairly clinical approach and cut out the preliminaries. You love beautiful, expensive things and have a strong dislike of gaudy or shoddy goods. Vulgarity has little appeal for you and loud music offends you. You are cultured, have good taste and enjoy reading.

As a parent You make a good, caring parent but like to impose your ideas on your children. You don't listen sufficiently to them so their aims and ideas can get pushed into the background. You are probably very proud of 'the old school tie', and want your children to attend the same school. You will have difficulty in accepting the chosen partners of your children, as nobody is ever considered good enough for them.

ORIGINAL

‛e Committee who
index of volunteers
Doubt hear from
Bourse. Our Principal

You have a creative, original mind, rich in ideas, as well as good visual sense and imagination. Invariably, you are animated but you are also a generally relaxed type who has no difficulty in relating with others. You may at times appear boisterous or even boastful, but are very big-hearted and always pleasant to have around. You can be greedy for sensation and have a love of the spectacular; at times you are emotional but you are predominantly charming, with an excellent visual memory.

In business Providing you are employed in an artistic field you do extremely well. Your artistic leanings, visual mind and love of colour can lead you into jobs involving design, creating patterns involving colour, producing book illustrations or book covers – all of these areas provide outlets for your talents. Often your type work in less creative jobs, but if you have outlets in your hobbies for your many talents, you will enjoy life; otherwise you can become quite depressed.

As a lover You have plenty of imagination and a colourful and light-hearted approach to life. You become depressed in tasteless surroundings and are at your most exuberant when surrounded by what you consider beautiful. A nature-lover, you love a partner to share the changing faces of the seasons with you. Your mind is rich in ideas and you can be adventurous and daring. Never one to conform, you find pleasure in exploring life and originality, either alone or with a chosen partner. Colour means a great deal to you and you will attempt to influence partners in their choice of clothes. You are warm, and ardent with the right partner, but will get rid of a possessive or limiting one. Sometimes you are awkward in social situations and dwell on the unimportant.

As a parent You probably consider your children wonderful creations of nature and will expose them to creative pursuits. Strict organization has little appeal for you, so getting the children to bed at a reasonable hour, or feeding them on time, will not be an issue; nor are you terribly practical. Hugs and kisses will rarely be in short supply but goodies for the packed lunch might be!

LOOPY

Please find enclosed my cheque. I hope we will meet soon.

The dominance of loops indicates a very emotional person: not only do you respond in an emotional fashion but you need an emotional response from others. This can seem vain, immature and hypersensitive, but it also indicates a sympathetic and compassionate nature. You may appear to be extroverted while actually feeling insecure inside. You are talkative, impulsive and hedonistic.

In business You become deeply involved, whether it be

with customers, patients or colleagues, and find it difficult to maintain the boundary between your business and personal lives. Since you talk too much, you are not suited to positions where confidentiality is an important requirement; you loathe solitary occupations and need to be surrounded by others. You are undoubtedly gifted with a good degree of intelligence but you dislike work where intense concentration is required. You waver between caution and independence and can be difficult to pin down.

As a lover The wider the loops of your script, the more gregarious and pleasure-seeking you are. You have a great need to be loved and find life barren if you aren't at the core of someone's existence. You love having a fuss made of you romantically. You also love music, movement, dancing and rhythm. Sexually you are very experimental – more or less anything goes. But you can be emotionally draining to your partner, wanting their full attention. Basically you are only attracted to very lively personalities and find the quiet type boring.

As a parent Full of cuddles and giggles, you more often than not welcome and enjoy the whole experience of parenthood. You go overboard about your 'gifted' or 'very beautiful' children, but are always sympathetic to their difficulties and problems, and will encourage them to be adventurous. Their friends will be welcome in the home and happily entertained, with lavish parties on birthdays, and plenty of loud music. You will dash off impulsively on some pursuit and children may well have to wait till late evening for supper, but no one seems to mind; you don't live by the clock. It's a pretty relaxed household.

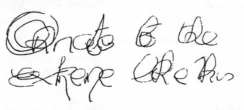

If your handwriting is fussy or tremendously elaborate, it shows an emphasis on unimportant things. You can be vulgar – wearing brash or tasteless clothes – and boastful. You may be lighthearted, but are also vain and conceited. You probably wear too much make-up, drive a mauve or pink car, and have a garden full of gnomes in every conceivable colour. You can be very generous and insist guests eat everything put down in front of them, but you will also ply them with drinks, heedless of the consequences of drinking too much. You are adventurous, and always kind to your friends – but ghastly if you don't like someone, and often a noisy neighbour.

In business Best left to your own devices, you are almost certainly most suited to self-employment. You are likely to be at the races when an important meeting is being held and will even wonder why it cannot be changed to fit in with your social needs. Very ostentatious, you are boastful and tell wild stories; you are certainly not the most honest and are good at bending the truth. Your colleagues will always have a good time with you but will rarely trust you.

As a lover Do you wear very low-cut dresses or underwear saying 'welcome'? Maybe even condoms that smell of strawberries or liquorice? Maybe you paint all your nails a different colour. Your type has a bawdy sense of humour and you are fond of playing practical jokes which can be tasteless. Does innuendo creep into every word you utter? Are you very generous, sending 200 red roses to the one you love when they could far more easily accommodate a dozen? These are all acts of an extremely ornate writer. You will certainly embarrass your friends but, if they are the same type you could all be in for an interesting time. There is always fun in the bedroom, but not necessarily of an appropriate nature!

As a parent   Your children will tend to look like a mini-Mum or Dad, dressed to kill in all the latest fashions and the gaudiest colours. You'll lavish pocket money on them and they will learn at an early age to spend, spend, spend. Not much discipline is exercised in this home and children learn not to show much consideration to others; their manners are frequently sadly lacking. More often than not, they are encouraged to partake in a large range of activities.

8

Width of Strokes

Broadness   n m

Narrowness   n m

BROADNESS

I absolutely don't
as what to write but
I try to put something

Broadness reveals someone who is expansive in social situations but can be quite contained in other areas of their life. You tend to be vivacious, sympathetic and generous, with broad views and a need to be free and unfettered. You are the world's best traveller and enjoy the whole experience, right from the moment you start your packing. Faraway places have great appeal – you feel drawn to the world and open spaces; you also need large rooms in which to spread yourself, and invariably have many and varied interests and hobbies. You can be very talkative and exaggerate stories. You like good clothes and enjoy mixed company. You are very frank, and friendly and helpful to those around you. You are also susceptible to others' charm.

In business The 9-to-5 type job is not for you, as you become extremely restless in this suitation. You give a great deal of consideration to the claims of others around you, helping colleagues whenever possible. Your aim in life is to be as good at your work as you can possibly be; you are deeply affected by failure and are driven to perfection by success. You have a good imagination but your ability to concentrate wavers: when it is good, it is extremely good, but at other times it is weak. Your eye for beauty often leads you to the world of design, fashion, and beauty, especially when travel is involved, but watch for a tendency to exceed your budget.

As a lover Adventurous and broadminded, your motto might be 'anything goes'! You easily attract others but are difficult to hang on to; you need romance, excitement and variety. Your ability to mix well makes it easy for you to associate with all types, from the penniless artist or writer to the successful head of an organization. Your impatience can get you into trouble. You will require a lot from your partner in terms of luxuries, but you are very generous, too – to your partner, friends and family, mentally and materially, and in all ways.

As a parent A child of yours is likely to be strapped to your chest when only a few weeks old, and shown the beauty of nature and the outside world. Exploration is what life is all about and this idea will be instilled in your offspring. They will be taken to restaurants, cinemas theatres, and concerts at an early age. The neighbours' children will be welcome in your home as well, and your children will enjoy a lively home life.

I am rather shy. I like going to
see the sort of people who have
and I play in an orchestra. My
reluting but I can't afford it
is to learn to ski. I have a

To understand the character of a person with a very narrow script it is easiest to think of a curtain pulled back very tightly. You are narrow-minded, with narrow visions and a controlled personality. You limit yourself unnecessarily due to fear: the car might break down, the weather might change, the train will not get into the station on time. Your introversion is related to your inhibitions, which give rise to cautiousness and feelings of timidity and loneliness. You want everything neat and tidy and are either economical or just plain mean, avoiding unnecessary expense and hoarding whatever you can. Narrowness means the emotions are directed inwards, and you lose out on many of the joys of life.

In business You restrict yourself greatly and are frequently distrustful of the moods and motives of others. You do have a marked sense of duty and will stick rigidly to your promises. You work to a well-devised, predetermined plan and have great difficulty with improvising. You are very self-conscious and have a strong dislike of being observed when working. Both critical and analytical, you tend to work best in a technical capacity. You have strong ethical leanings.

As a lover Your sensitivity gives rise to problems and you behave in a modest and reserved manner. Your love-making can be quite mechanical and restrained, as your narrow-mindedness restricts any form of adventurous behaviour. Your lover will have few surprises, sexually or otherwise. You can be so predictable that bedtime boredom easily settles in. Nor do you have a flair for gift-giving. Sadly, a poverty of ideas does not help, but a warm, affectionate partner could.

As a parent You love your children but are over-protective, cautious and limiting. Your home will be beautifully kept, and your children will be well fed and clothed, but restricted in their movements. You may be too fearful to allow them to travel by train, go on school outings or stay at friends' homes for the night. However, these concerns are borne of an admirable, marked sense of duty to your children.

Pressure on Stroke

ᴧ ᴧ ᴧ ᴧ ᴧ ᴧ ᴧ ᴧ ᴧ

Assessing Pressure

The degree of force can be judged by feeling an original sample of writing between your thumb and index finger. Strong indentation indicates heavy pressure; slight indentation indicates medium; no indentation indicates light. Pasty pressure looks heavy but has no indentation, and is frequently produced by a felt tip or broad nib. Light pressure with pointed tops is classified as sharp, and varying is a combination of both light and heavy.

HEAVY

It has been a pleasure you, and I hope you

Heavy pressure reveals a forceful personality with a great deal of energy available. No 'shrinking violet', you need to make an impression and are easily excited to action. You are not easily discouraged and can inspire others. Challenges are welcome, as is material reward for your efforts. Essentially you are materialistic, strong-willed and stubborn. Your remarkable energy is accompanied by great stamina, and you love change, new surroundings and active people. You can, however, be morose or given to depression. There is a tendency to indulge in anti-social or aggressive behaviour if you have insufficient outlet for your energies.

In business Powerful, strong and hard working, you welcome all new challenges with delight. You might be an excellent managing director or a particularly good salesperson. Rejection doesn't worry you unduly; you just go back for more. You can be both harsh and stern and sometimes others find it difficult to get along with you, but you are respected for your abilities and forceful attitudes: you certainly make your presence felt.

As a lover Extremely warm, ardent and demanding, you love company and can be tiring in your thirst for new experiences and love of activity. You need outlets for your physical energy, and your personality type often make good sports people. You enjoy wining and dining, travel, and are a very interesting companion, but you do demand attention. Sexually you are adventurous, extremely tactile and sensual. When frustrated you can be very aggressive.

As a parent You chivvy the family into activity but take your role as a provider very seriously. You like the trappings of wealth: big house, car, holidays, good education, and more. You can be intolerant and very stubborn, so the family tends to go along with your ideas. Your strong idealism can put pressure on your partner and offspring. Yours is never a boring household, and an unadventur-

65

ous partner would never survive in this relationship. You can be aggressive, or even cruel, to your offspring.

MEDIUM

I used to buy pens all the time, usually fountain pens so that

This pressure is the most common one seen, and an indication of a reasonable degree of energy and vitality. If you use medium pressure, you are the adaptable type, with a primary interest in people, and a secondary interest in material things. You have sufficient willpower to overcome problems or obstacles on a day-to-day basis and do not try to impose your will on others.

In business You have a reasonable drive and do not necessarily want to extend yourself too far. As you are both adaptable and composed you tend to be popular with your colleagues. You listen to and help others: people-handling is one of your gifts.

As a lover Providing you do not have an over-demanding partner, you are loving, caring and pleasant. You enjoy most things in moderation and are consistent in your behaviour. There is no point in others surprising you with expensive gifts; you will only worry about the extravagance of the deed!

As a parent Nurturing and thoughtful, you will expect only what you consider the children are capable of. You will get to know other parents and help at school fêtes and the like. You are considered nice but unadventurous.

When I returned to the city, where I had been born, after many years of absence I was dismayed to find that many of it's narrow streets had been.

Light pressure shows a person with low energy levels and stamina. You are sensitive and greatly affected by things others do and say. You take offence easily, even when none was intended. You have a certain delicacy of feeling and can be greatly upset by violence and swearing, on television or elsewhere in your environment. You loathe loud noises, blaring radios, rough behaviour and harsh words. You may experience difficulty in learning from past experiences and tend to repeat your mistakes. You are likely to be idealistic, with an interest in spiritual development, refined, gentle and sensitive to beauty, art and music.

In business You are at your best working in a creative field and, being very idealistic, set high standards for yourself. If you choose to work in a sales organization you will have the necessary intelligence, but as you are not aggressive you will have to work twice as hard as the person who writes with heavy pressure, as those writers more naturally succeed in this area. This type of work could take its toll on your delicate nature and result in your being rather tense and nervous. Your thoughts and feelings are intense, but they do not last for long. You would make a good television or theatre critic.

As a lover You are extremely gentle and tender. As you love the arts, you will want a partner who will accompany you to art galleries, theatres, concerts, and the like. Your sensitive nature needs careful handling and you take offence if for some reason an arrangement is cancelled.

You have a low tolerance for alcohol, so should not over-indulge; neither do you react well to shock or drugs. Your love of beauty is tremendous and, if you find the right person, you will treat them like a precious object. The sex will be sparing but very tender.

As a parent You encourage your children to behave beautifully at all times, to show consideration for others and refrain from shouting or raising their voices. Your children grow up aware of many cultural pursuits and will consider this a normal way of life. You will welcome the 'right' friends for your children into your home, but you will be very selective. Often the children of your personality type are successful as actors, since they experience little difficulty in taking on the character of another person while leaving their own hidden.

PASTY

I would like to study graphology further. Is there a course offered here in

A pasty pressure appears heavy, but is in fact light. The heavy look is produced by a felt-tip or broad-nibbed pen consciously chosen for its effect, and the style is always indicative of a marked prevalence of sensual traits. You delight in creature comforts that stimulate the five senses: perfume, food and drink, touching, music and movement. You have a deep appreciation of the present moment but also welcome new experiences. You exhibit genuine warmth and a good sense of humour. You try to make life fun and are a very good companion. You are deeply emotional and carry the scars of hurt or happiness for a long time. You need richness and luxury in your life but hate losing money. You are a nature lover with particular love of flowers and trees.

In business You usually delight in a free and easy disposition which enables you to get along very well with colleagues. Your deep appreciation of colour and a marked aptitude for working with it would make you an excellent photographer, designer, or artist. You have a gifted imagination and an ability to visualize. But this can lead to day-dreaming or, on other occasions, burning out by endeavouring to do too much at once.

As a lover You are extremely warm, sensual and ardent. Dining out or cooking exotic meals at home plays an important part in your routine. Good wines are also greatly appreciated but – a word of warning – you can be given to excesses! Walking in the woods by moonlight or tramping through the countryside all have appeal. You look on the positive side of life and have a great sense of fun. You will surprise your lover with well-chosen gifts at any time: 'Why wait for birthdays?' is your attitude. You need tasteful surroundings and attractive companions. But keep away from casinos – you hate losing! You're a very sexy partner, who enjoys buying a lover flowers or perfume.

As a parent You are very interested in your offspring and will delight in taking them for nature rambles (imparting information as you go), or sailing trips and travel at home and abroad. You give generously of your time, feelings and ideas, exuding warmth and offering plenty of kisses and cuddles. Yours may not be the most organized household but it's among the happiest. Here, the children are always encouraged to use their imaginations.

All good men come to
the and of the
past

You experience emotions intellectually rather than with
the whole body. You tend to be hypersensitive and nervous, an idealist with very high morals and principles,
and you see things as right or wrong, good or bad, pure
or sordid. When you choose to communicate you are articulate and rapid in speech. You are a deep thinker but
your feelings are not long-lasting. You may be spiritual,
and are very sensitive to beauty in all its forms. You don't
have an abundance of energy but tend to save it for when
it is necessary. Scepticism and an analytical mind are other
character traits found in your type. You can be extremely
critical, with a hasty temper.

In business On the whole, you are clever, critical and
logical. You set very high standards and are never content with low work-standards or poor time-keeping. You
can subdue colleagues with a particular sense of humour
that shows considerable irony and sarcasm. Under pressure, you become extremely irritable and nervous, so are
best left to work at your own pace. You would make an
excellent theatre or film critic; many clergymen and women
produce this type of stroke.

As a lover You place a lot more emphasis on the importance of mental processes than emotions. You are very
conscious of hygiene and dislike anything you might con-

sider 'dirty'. You are not prone to over-indulgence in food, drink or sex, and you have a low tolerance for shock and drugs. You can be cold, remote and restrained. You are very selective in those you associate with and have a great dislike of any form of loudness or vulgarity. Sex, too, will be a matter for restraint.

As a parent Your children will be expected to obey all the household rules without question. If they follow the same refined, cultural pursuits that you do, everyone will be happy; but should the children be interested in more boisterous activities, you will show total disinterest. Energy is reserved in this family for what is considered refined, decent and respectable – with little room for manoeuvre! Hasty tempers do flare from time to time. An immaculately kept home is very important to you.

VARYING

told that sloping letters : shows signs of distrust ing upright !

If your handwriting is light on some strokes and heavy on others, it shows a personality that is still in the process of growth – varying between idealism and materialism, ardour and restraint. You can be optimistic one day and pessimistic the next. The majority of us develop one particular pressure eventually.

G. Bernard Shaw   Anne

Best wishes —
Sue Lawley.   Alexandra

Margaret

Elizabeth R   Mark Phillips

Picasso   Elvis Presley   Gary Titeth

Iza Goddard

Jacqueline Kennedy   Love   Paul McCartney

Sincerely
Bette Davis

Anita Dobson

Hugh M Hefner   WALT DISNEY   Tessa Sanderson

SECTION II

Secondary Movements

10

The Personal Pronoun: 'I'

	Form	Indicates
1	Printed	Clear thinking, good taste, confidence
2	Small (either printed or cursive)	Lack of confidence, a feeling of being hard done by
3	Very tall	Confidence and pride
4	Single stroke	Intelligence, independent thinking
5	Narrow loop	Idealism and emotional control
6	Average loop	Emotional well-being and good willpower
7	Very wide loop	Emotionalism, vanity and pride
8	Closed	Total absorption in self

9		Arc to left	Great difficulty in taking responsibility
10		Pointed at top	Desire for explanations for everything and a probing mind
11		Like Fig. 4	Inflexibility; irritability and defensiveness
12		Like Fig. 7	Familiarity with figures and a love of material possessions
13		Like Fig. 9	Influence of the father and early life experiences
14		Like Fig. 2	Feeling of being second-rate and difficulty in relating intimately (often has a particularly clever brother or sister)
15		Small and cramped	Shyness and self-consciousness
16		Like small letter	Great immaturity and a crushed ego
17		Hook to the left	Aggressiveness and retention of negative feelings from the past
18		Like letter X	Fear of dying; fear of true nature being exposed

19		Triangular base	Hard and aggressive nature
20		Simplified with tick starting stroke	Concision and precision
21		Simplied with curved base	Independence and self-contentment
22		Amended	Temporary malaise and touchiness
23		Coiled	A love of self and a tendency towards greediness
24		Curved	Avoidance of involvement; can suggest hearing problems
25		Musical symbol	Musical appreciation or ability
26		Bowed to left	Invitation to others to treat you badly, either verbally or physically
27		Dropping below baseline	Insensitivity to partner's feelings; deceit
28		Top and bottom strokes disconnected	Active or passive participation in ball games

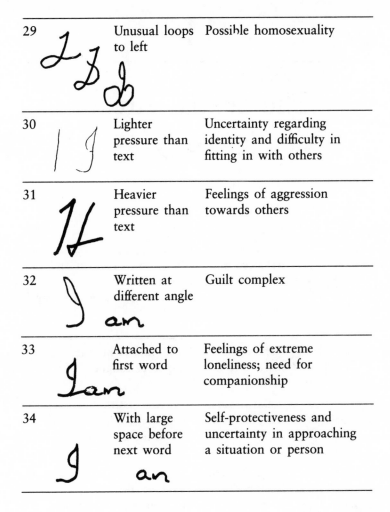

29	Unusual loops to left	Possible homosexuality
30	Lighter pressure than text	Uncertainty regarding identity and difficulty in fitting in with others
31	Heavier pressure than text	Feelings of aggression towards others
32	Written at different angle	Guilt complex
33	Attached to first word	Feelings of extreme loneliness; need for companionship
34	With large space before next word	Self-protectiveness and uncertainty in approaching a situation or person

11

The Sexual Area: 'g' & 'y'

		Form	Indicates
1	*g y*	Balanced and complete	Ability to be content and happy within one relationship; makes a loving partner
2	*q y g*	Very small lower stroke or loop	Little interest in sex; temporary fatigue
3	*g y*	Very narrow loop	Sexual repression; fear of commitment
4	*g y*	Very wide loop	Good sex drive and imagination; materialistic streak
5	*g y*	Unfinished loop	Flirtatious nature; lack of interest in the sex act
6	*g y*	Low crossing	Dissatisfaction with current partner

7	Swinging endstroke	Desire for constant change of partner
8	Long, straight stroke to left	Nature that derives a lot of pleasure from masturbation
9	Endstroke to left	Sublimated sexual urges; enjoyment in helping others
10	Small triangle	Sexual anxiety and frigidity, frustration
11	Large triangle	Sexual aggression combined with indifference to partner; tendency to leave partner frustrated
12	Very long, looped	Ease of emotional involvement; love of sporting activities
13	Hook to left	Avoidance of responsibility; will run from commitment
14	Completed figure 8 in lower zone	Possible homosexuality
15	Tick on endstroke	Need for encouragement and reassurance
16	Very heavy pressure and full loop	Sexually demanding nature (three times a day!)

17	Straight downstroke	Selfishness
18	Exaggerated lower zone movements	Active or latent homosexuality
19	Broken base	Sexual disappointment and fearful nature
20	Like a corkscrew	Inventiveness and imagination
21	Upstroke drops	Feeling of discouragement or anger towards partner
22	Loop on baseline	Sexual vanity (enjoys walking around naked)
23	Triangle in lower zone	Unresolved sexual anxiety; prudish nature
24	All y's and g's the same	Little imagination (every-Saturday-night type – preferably with the lights out)
25	Two or three varieties	Healthy, imaginative interest in sex

| 26 | Every *y* or *g* different | Easily stimulated nature; lack of control |

ૐૐૐૐૐૐ

12

Capital Letters

	Form	Indicates
1	Tall	Self-respect, self-reliance and a healthy degree of confidence
	Handwriting	*Analysis*
2	Very tall	Pride, vanity and conceit; mistaken confidence when starting on a new project
	Handwriting	*Analysis*
3	Short	Modesty, slight uncertainty and hesitation before undertaking anything new
	Handwriting	*Analysis*
4	Very short	Lack of confidence; humility and tendency to stick with the 'tried and trusted'
	Handwriting	*Analysis*

5	First hump larger	Pride and egoism
6	Second hump larger	Pride in family achievements; desire to be liked and accepted
7	End stroke extending under whole word	Expectation that others will hang on your every word; self-satisfaction
8	Extremely simplified	Ability to see essentials instantly; individualism, creativity, structural ability
9	Very broad	Generosity, open-mindedness and love of freedom
10	Very narrow	Uptight, reserved, careful nature, lacking in spontaneity
11	Printed capitals with cursive writing	Clear thinking; desire to get on with whatever is of interest at this moment
12	Large loop at beginning	Pomposity and a desire for attention (found in the writing of actors, politicians and salespeople)

13	Extended top stroke	Enterprising nature with a love of challenges
14	Starting with an additional stroke	Difficulty getting along with others; tendency towards obstruction
15	Starting stroke over whole word	Protective nature, especially with friends, family and colleagues
16	No starting stroke	Practicality; directness
17	Long, straight starting stroke	Resentment; tendency to blame others for misfortune
18	Garland starting stroke	Warmth, affection, caring nature with a desire for acceptance
19	Arcade starting stroke	Nature that is secretive, slow to change, traditional

20	Angled starting stroke	Aggression, feeling of being cheated; hostility

Dry (handwritten)

21	Space after capital	Observant nature with the ability to sense atmosphere

Space after Capital (handwritten)

13

Small Letters

	Form	Indicates
1	Variations of the same letter in a piece of writing	Versatility and adaptability ⱤRS ◠ a ꙅ e Ɛ
2	Missing letter in the middle of a word Crᴣy brve	Distraction, poor concentration; individual under pressure = Crazy = brave
3	Missing letter at end of word centr modes	Mind working faster than the pen on paper; a desire to move on to next interest or project; impatience = centre = modest
4	Letters decreasing at end of word decreasing	Tact and diplomacy; ability to keep a secret

5	Letters increasing at end of word	Blabbermouth; gossip

increasing

6	Capital in the middle of a word	Mistaken or confused priorities

ciRcles

7	A mixture of print and cursive	Social insecurity; sparing communication and discomfort in large groups

tys print like this if it's my to a close friend. However,

8	A mixture of broad and narrow letters	Broadmindedness, generosity alternating with nervousness, meanness

Now is the time

9	Reversed letters	Antisocial behaviour and a dislike of normal rules, regulations and people in authority

d = 6   s = 2   k = ʎ

10	Strokes that fall below the line	Stubbornness, obstinacy and firm convictions

d ʒ k

11	Elaborate letters	Vulgarity, coarseness and noisiness

12	Letters tied in knots	Inflexibility

13	Lasso loops on letters	Poetic, childlike but pleasant nature

14	Curly strokes	Great sense of humour and a sense of the ridiculous

15	Angular letters	Determination, mathematical ability, thoroughness

16	Unusual letter formations	Originality, creativity and individualism

17	Ink-filled letters	Nature given to excesses; possibility of violence

18	Spiky tops	Probing mind, argumentative streak

| 19 | Very small *i* in relation to other letters | Kindness; a feeling of self-pity (often found in the handwriting of nurses and carers) |

Very tiny

| 20 | With double letters, second taller than first | Ability to command respect on entering a room (teachers, lecturers) |

el tt

| 21 | Very large *a* and *o* in relation to other letters | Jealousy and possessiveness in relationships |

cOmparison

| 22 | Double circles on *a* and *o* | Tendency to be hypocritical and devious; possibility of dishonesty |

a o

| 23 | Letters open on baseline | Flexible morals; lack of trustworthiness |

a o b

| 24 | Very tall upper zone movements | Pride, high ideals and imagination |

tall like this

25	Very low upper zone movements	Lack of imagination; dull personality

small like this

26	Constant amendments that do nothing to aid legibility	Neurotic tendencies; fear and suspicion

d   t   ℓ   m

27	Letters like figures	Mathematical ability; good judgement.

g = 9   r = 2

t = 7   y = 4

28 ε ∂	Greek *e* and *d*	Refinement, culture (often found in the handwriting of writers and journalists)
29 ɷ ɷ	Extra loops on *m* and *n*	False charm and flattery; also a concern for others
30 ɑ ɔ	*a* and *o* open to left	Tendency to speak about others behind their back
31 ɑ o	*a* and *o* open to right	Open and direct nature
32 ∂ ∂	*d* curled back	Self-protectiveness; speedy replies

14

i Dots

		Form	Indicates
1	ɩ̇	Directly above	Precision, accuracy
2	ɩ	To the right	Impulsiveness, impatience
3	ɩ	To the left	Procrastination and caution
4	ɩ	Omitted	Lack of attention to detail, carelessness
5	ɩ	Very high	Curiosity, observant person
6	ɩ	Arcade	Secretiveness, control
7	ɩ ɩ	Like dash	Hasty temper, irritability and sarcasm
8	ɩ	Wavy	Fun-loving nature

9	. L	Light	Weak will; lack of energy
10	i L (very heavy)	Very heavy	Strong will, overbearing nature
11	◢ L	Club shape	Aggression, cruelty
12	o i L	Circle	Attention-seeking, slight eccentricity (often found in the writing of people who enjoy working with their hands - artists and craftsmen, physiotherapists, hairdressers, chefs, etc.)
13	ᒻ ᒻ ᒻ ᒻ ᒻ	Varying	Inconsistent behaviour and work patterns; liking for change and variety

15

t Crosses

	Form		Indicates
1	∫	Cross omitted	Carelessness, absent-mindedness
2	t	Low cross	Difficulty in overcoming day-to-day obstacles; caution
3	t	Medium	Conscientiousness and courage
4	t	High	Bravery and tenacity
5	ʇ	To the left	Procrastination
6	ⱻ	Low cross away from stem	Acceptance of challenge, impatience
7	ⱻ	Middle cross away from stem	Drive, initiative and impatience
8	⌐	High cross away from stem	Leader who takes charge

9		Pointing down	Contrary and obstinate nature
10		Cruciform	Fatalism; religious leanings
11		Very heavy pressure	Energy, domineering, selfishness
12		Very light pressure	Weak will, lack of confidence
13		Double cross	Obsessive nature with the inclination to recheck everything
14		Cross above the stem	Someone with their head in the clouds; lack of realism
15		Looped	Sensitivity, vanity
16		Wavy	Sense of humour and fun; a mimic
17		Club-like	Bad-temper and cruelty
18		Upward curve	Quick mind but very critical
19		Angled	Obstinacy, stubbornness; strong opinions
20		Loop knot	Persistence and love of challenge

21		Long stroke across double *t*	Protective towards family and friends
22		Convex	Self-discipline
23		Concave	Self-indulgence
24		Varying	Unreliable willpower and control; versatility and the ability to improvise

16

Line Spacing

AVERAGE

*currently at university after
enter journalism as my chosen
lthough I have nine 'o' levels*

Normal spacing shows the ability to think clearly and explain things to other people. You are discriminating in what you do and in your choice of friends. You invariably have a sympathetic nature and are a good judge of character.

WIDE

*n Sunday the 9th October I
enerife with a friend, on
derstand that you are the*

You fear closeness with others and tend to set yourself above other people. You can create grandiose fantasies and put yourself on a pedestal; alternatively, you may just harbour distrust and suspicions. You make extravagant gestures from time to time to other people, and are also frequently generous to yourself.

NARROW

[handwritten text:]

> I you know for
> - the standard of
> ence, Memory, vitality,
> bilities, interests, etc.,
> revealed through

You suffer from confused thoughts and ideas. The more the lines run into each other, the more confused your personality. You are constantly in need of expressing your thoughts and ideas but experience great difficulty in putting them into action. Your concentration is not good and you are prone to accidents. You are lively and forceful but you lack clarity of purpose. You may be tight-fisted.

17

Word Spacing

WELL BALANCED

It position and & w
a report on him. Res sec
are pre eminant. He wil

Your writing shows clarity of thinking and inner organization, an ability to deal flexibly with others and handle your own thoughts and feelings well. You are methodical and opportunist. You strive to express yourself clearly and can become irritated if misunderstood. Intelligence, maturity, good planning and good judgement are clearly shown here.

WIDE

Mary had a little lam
Its feet were white a
And everywhere that

You loathe living in close proximity to others for fear of others breathing down your neck. You are selective in everything, from your choice of friends to tasks in hand. Others can find you aloof or at least reserved. You normally show courage, independence and generosity. You dislike asking others for favours and prefer to make your own decisions. You show a tendency to isolate yourself and believe, correctly or incorrectly, that you have difficulty in communicating with others. You will commit yourself to issues or projects you consider appropriate, rather than accepting what others try to force upon you.

NARROW

last year at college doing a degree
we applied to firms for a
ing However I don't know if

You are excessively friendly and may compete with others for attention. You mix indiscriminately and hate being left alone, even for reasonably short periods of time. You can often be very selfish, expecting others to give readily of their time while you are not prepared to do likewise. Impulsive, you will intrude on conversations, expecting to be welcomed. Tact is not your strong point. You over-extend yourself in all areas of your life.

VERY UNEVEN

I have just returned from San
with an artist and a ps
thing quite interesting

You are rather hesitant and unsure of how to behave or what path to follow. You may seem rather arrogant, but

99

this is a cover-up for your confused thoughts and ideas. At times you are friendly, at other times less so. You do not plan well and tend to fall into situations. You are difficult to organize, and often join clubs or committees on a whim, only to decide later that this is not what you really want.

18

Margins

BALANCED

PERHAPS I
SHOULD PHONE
ROBERT TO
MAKE SURE

You have a self-assured personality and know how to adjust to fit in with prevailing circumstances. You handle your relationships well.

WIDE LEFT

I LIKE TO SIT
WRITE BUT I
AM ALWAYS
IN A HURRY
RUSH, RUSH

You are attempting to move forward and are communicative. The future is more important to you than the past; you try to learn from past experiences and mistakes.

WIDE RIGHT

> I RESIST
> CHANGE AND
> LIKE TO PLAN
> WELL IN
> ADVANCE FOR
> EVERYTHING
> I DO.

Tomorrow scares you a little and you like to plan things well in advance. You are uncertain of the future and resist change. Your sensitivity holds you back and you will stay in unsuitable relationships for fear of ending up on your own.

WIDE MARGINS ALL ROUND

> I DO FEEL
> ISOLATED BUT
> DO NOTHING
> ABOUT IT!

You feel isolated and need to get out more and meet new people. You are confined in too small a range of interests and need to be less concerned about holding on to things and more interested in extending yourself.

ABSENCE OF MARGINS / WRITING
IN THE MARGINS

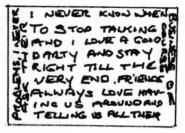

You are intrusive and do not recognize barriers between yourself and other people. At times, you become excitable and verbose. Give others their space and back off occasionally; not everybody can love you. You have a well-developed sense of economy.

DEEP TOP

You show respect for the feelings of others. Good timekeeping is important to you as you do not care to inconvenience others. You are quite formal, even reserved. You need to spend some time alone.

WHAT SHALL I
DO TODAY? I
JUST DON'T KNOW
MAYBE I SHALL
DECIDE LATER.

Your interest in other people quickly dissipates and you avoid commitment. You can be both idealistic and aloof, take offence much too readily and behave in a very sensitive manner. You don't always know what you want.

19

Signatures

A signature cannot be analysed on its own, but must always be examined in relation to the body of the script, as people often imitate the signature of someone they admire. An assumed signature frequently projects an image an individual would like to present to the world, and movements that appeal can be maintained for the extent of the signature but not for longer periods of time. People who sign many cheques or contracts may deform their signature, deliberately or unconsciously, to make it difficult for others to copy; similarly, those who sign vast amounts of correspondence may abbreviate their signature for speed.

	Form	*Indicates*
1	Text and signature identical	Lack of façade; the same behaviour in public and private

to know more about

I buy & are they esp

Wilson

2	Larger	Uncertain ego; pretence of being extroverted

This is my usual script

Diana Jones

3	Smaller	A pretence of modesty; quiet confidence

Do you want this?

Pamela Bridges

4	First name and surname connected	An ability to project your personality well; memorable character

Joan Collins

5	Rising	Professional ambition and drive

Pamela Joan Ingram

6	Falling	Negative frame of mind

Brenda Potts

| 7 | Single underline | Love of being noticed; a fair degree of confidence |

John Howard

| 8 | Double underline | Desire for recognition, love of an audience |

Paul Winter

| 9 | Wavy underline | Fair degree of confidence without the expectation of being taken seriously |

Sharon Brown

| 10 | Light full stop | Liking for the last word; caution |

Nancy Thomas.

| 11 | Heavy full stop | Insistence on having the last word; stubbornness |

Julia Brackit.

| 12 | Two full stops | Love of a good argument; a need to have the last word |

P. J. Dodds..

| 13 | Encircled | Pushy, secretive nature with a desire to outwit others |

Reg Wilson

| 14 | Letters decrease in size | Tact and diplomacy; consideration for others |

Robert Dunn

| 15 | Letters increase in size | Impulsiveness and tactlessness |

Mary Hacker

| 16 | Very broad | Need for space; intrepid qualities |

Alec Harrison

17	Very narrow	Fear, tension and nervousness

Pamela Bridges

18	Extended endstroke	Distrust of the moods and motives of colleagues or friends

Eileen Moran

19	Long garland starting stroke	Difficulty in getting down to a task; feelings of uncertainty

Philip Sawyer

20	Long angular starting stroke	Resentful; blaming

David Evan

21	Very large capitals	Great pride and idealism

Catherine Patterson

22	Small middle initial	Dislike of middle name

Amy B. Green

23	Small first initial	Personal uncertainty; reliance on social status for recognition

H. Hughes.

24	Large first initial	Greater emphasis on self than partner; often suggests an unhappy relationship

Joe Lyons

25	Right slant text – left slant signature	Self-doubt and time wasting (usually temporary)

to the right

. Janice Holmes

26	Left slant text – right slant signature	Outward confidence but inward uncertainty

I write like this

Robert Dooley

27	Slanting in all directions	Moodiness, uncertainty and provocativeness

Paddy Murphy

| 28 | Overly ornate in relation to the text | An exaggerated sense of own importance; not always truthful |

Just ordinary script
Evelyn Major

| 29 | Simplified in relation to the text | Verbose and evasive; a tricky combination |

Kinda Elaborated.
Jessie James

| 30 | Heavier pressure than text | Willingness to strive for what you want |

Light Pressure
P.J. Lyons

| 31 | Lighter pressure than text | Diminishing momentum |

Very Heavy
a. J. Smith

| 32 | Use of full first name rather than initial | Attempt to break down initial barrier in getting acquainted; a friendly disposition |

Mary Evans

Elizabeth Taylor

Charles

John Major

Jimmy Savile

Andrew

Philip

Margaret Thatcher

Dustin Hoffman

Warm regards

John Wayne

Diana.

Sarah Ferguson.

Judith Chalmers

112